nihongo notes 6
situational japanese 1

by osamu mizutani
nobuko mizutani

The Japan Times

First edition: November 1984
Fifth printing: July 1990

Jacket design by Koji Detake

ISBN4-7890-0253-5

Published by The Japan Times, Ltd.
5-4, Shibaura 4-chome, Minato-ku, Tokyo 108, Japan

Printed in Japan

FOREWORD

This book is a compilation of 74 columns appearing in *The Japan Times* from April 17, 1983 to September 9, 1984. (The preceding 350 columns have been published as *Nihongo Notes 1, 2, 3, 4* and *5*.)

It is a great pleasure for us to be able to publish another volume, and we are very grateful for your continued interest. We hope that you will enjoy reading this volume and that it will help you to understand the Japanese language more fully.

While continuing to explain the actual usage of various Japanese expressions, we have changed the format slightly from this volume on to focus on how Japanese is used in specific situations and for specific purposes. In other words, we have shifted the emphasis from an expression-oriented approach to a situation-oriented one. The famous Mr. Lerner has advanced from being a poor, earnest learner who continually stumbles in his efforts to communicate in Japanese to a keen observer of how the Japanese language is used who introduces the situations.

In this volume, we have attempted to explain, among other things, how the Japanese meet, part, introduce others, make requests politely, and express reserve towards others; namely, we have concentrated on explaining how the Japanese language is used in social situations.

We would like to acknowledge the help of Janet Ashby, who checked the English for these columns and offered valuable suggestions just as she did for the preceding five volumes.

October, 1984
Osamu and Nobuko Mizutani

CONTENTS

Being introduced 8
Referring to a mutual acquaintance when
    being introduced 10
Referring to previous meetings 12
Parting from someone you meet every day .. 14
Parting from family members 16
Putting an end to telephone conversations 18
Starting a business discussion 20
Ordering a meal at a restaurant 22
Visiting someone without notice 24
Giving reasons for making a request 26
Introducing oneself as someone's family
    member 28
Offering a gift 30
Asking someone to return a phone call 32
Conveying a message 34
Declining an offer of help 36
Expressing gratitude for help 38
Making explanations 40
Responding to a compliment 42
Describing physical problems —
    stomachache 44
Describing physical troubles — headache 46
Describing physical problems — being hurt
    in a fall 48
Honno — Signaling devaluation 50
Tazunete-kuru — Describing actions directed
    at the speaker 52
Hito-ni osareru — Suffering from soneone's
    actions 54
Migi-ni magarimasu — Giving directions 56
Doo sureba yoroshii-deshoo — Asking for
    instructions 58

Arakajime yoyaku-suru — Redundancy 60

Otsukaresama used as an expression of
  meeting and parting 62

Endoo or *Endoo-mame* — Changes in the
  meaning of words 64

Saremasu-ka —Expression of respect 66

Soryaa . . . — An indication of one's opinion . 68

. . . te-imasen used to indicate incompletion . 70

. . . te form used to indicate a reason 72

. . . ta used to indicate the completion of an
  action 74

noni used to indicate unexpectedness or
  dissatisfaction 76

Watashi-ga vs. *Watashi-wa* 78

. . . te used to end a sentence 80

. . . na used for the negative imperative 82

. . . na used for a familiar command 84

. . . te-wa used for indicating condition 86

Chan-to used to express expectations 88

Expressions of pleasure 90

Suru used to mean 'to cost' 92

Moshika-suru-to used to indicate uncertainty . 94

desu-mono used to mean 'since' or 'for' 96

koto used to mean 'necessity' 98

tokoro used to mean 'situation' 100

Referring to someone else's wishes 102

. . . te-itadaku to express gratitude 104

Some contracted forms in rapid speech 106

Sochira, kochira used as personal pronouns ... 108

. . . ppoi used to mean '. . . ish' 110

. . . dasu used to mean 'start . . . ing' 112

Expressions meaning 'Not all . . . ' 114

Expressions used for strong denial 116

Hanasu (speak) and *hanashikakeru* (speak
  to) 118

Expressions ending in . . . *nasai* 120

. . . *komu* used to mean 'into' 122

Use of . . . *desu,* . . . *deshita* 124

. . . *no koto-desu-ga* used when starting a
statement 126

Some words used for counting things 128

Signals to indicate that one is going to start
talking 130

The first part of a sentence implying the
rest 132

Haitte-iru vs. *irete-aru* 134

Sore-de vs. *sore-dewa* 136

Negation of a reason 138

Pittari, sutto, etc. — the use of mimicry
words 140

The intonation of *Soo-desu-ka* 142

Tomo and *mochiron* used for emphasis. 144

Ohirudemo tabemashoo-ka — Indirect
expressions 146

ka used to show reserve 148

The difference between *sono* and *ano* 150

Expressions indicating the subject 152

Common sayings and fixed numbers of
syllables 154

Note Concerning Romanization

The romanization used in this book (as well as in *An Introduction to Modern Japanese*) is based on the Hepburn system with the following modifications.

1. When the same vowel occurs consecutively, the letter is repeated rather than using the "-" mark.

    ex. *Tookyoo*   (instead of *Tōkyō*)

2. The sound indicated by the hiragana ん is written with "*n*" regardless of what sound follows it.

    ex. *shinbun*   (instead of *shimbun*)

    ex. *shinpai*   (instead of *shimpai*)

The words connected with hyphens are pronounced as one unit.

    ex. *genki-desu*

    ex. *Soo-desu-ne*

Being introduced

The other day Mr. Takada introduced Mr. Lerner to a Mr. Yamada, and the conversation went as follows:

Takada: *Yamada-san, kochira-wa Raanaa-san-desu.*

(Mr. Yamada, this is Mr. Lerner.)

Lerner: *Hajimemashite. Raanaa-de-gozaimasu.*
はじめまして。 ラーナーでございます。
Doozo yoroshiku.
どうぞ よろしく。
(How do you do? My name is Lerner. Glad to meet you.)

Yamada: *Kochira-koso doozo yoroshiku.*
こちらこそ どうぞ よろしく。
(The pleasure is mine, Mr. Lerner.)

Later Mr. Lerner wondered if he had made the correct response.

*　　　*　　　*

Mr. Lerner could either give his own name, as in *Raanaa-de-gozaimasu,* or leave it out since Mr. Takada has already said it; it is more formal and polite to give it. When the other person has said *Doozo yoroshiku* to you first, it is appropriate to say *Kochira-koso doozo yoroshiku.*

The physical distance between the speakers is, generally speaking, greater in Japanese conversation than in English. This depends upon whether the speakers shake hands or bow; people stand closer when shaking hands than when bowing. Some Japanese shake hands but most of them tend to bow; especially women prefer bowing. It is best for you to observe how the Japanese you are talking with behave and act accordingly.

Very often name cards (*meeshi*) are exchanged while saying *Doozo yoroshiku.* When you receive one, you should express your thanks by saying *Arigatoo-gozaimasu* and study it. When you hand over your own name card, you should be careful to give it to the other person so that he can easily take it and read it without turning it around. When you don't have a name card to give him, you can say

Sumimasen-ga meeshi-no mochiawase-ga arimasen-de. . .

(Sorry, I happen to have no name cards with me.)

After being introduced in this way, the conversation will usually proceed to a discussion of the work, background or mutual friends of the speakers.

Referring to a mutual acquaintance when being introduced

When Mr. Lerner was introduced to Mr. Yamada, a friend of Mr. Takada's, after exchanging *Hajimemashite* (How do you do?), he felt that he should say something about his relations with Takada so that he could develop the conversation, and wondered what was the appropriate way of doing so.

* * *

When two people meet for the first time, referring to a mutual acquaintance serves as a good conversational opening. How they refer to him depends on his relations with the speaker and the listener.

In Mr. Lerner's case, for instance, if Mr. Takada is closer to him than to Mr. Yamada, he can be at ease in talking about his relations with Mr. Takada. He can say something like

Takada-san-towa zutto issho-ni shigoto-o shite-imasu.

(I have been working with Mr. Takada for a long time.)

Takada-san-towa yoku issho-ni nomimasu.

(Mr. Takada and I often go drinking together.)

On the other hand, if Mr. Takada is closer to Mr. Yamada than to himself, Mr. Lerner should express his gratitude to Mr. Takada, as in

Takada-san-niwa itsumo osewa-ni natte-imasu.
高田さんには　いつも　おせわに　なっています。
(Mr. Takada is always kind to me.)

Takada-san-niwa iroiro oshiete-itadaite-imasu.

(Mr. Takada helps me a great deal. — *lit.* He

teaches me many things.)

He can express his desire to establish good relations with Mr. Yamada by thanking Mr. Takada, whom he identifies with Mr. Yamada.

This can be more clearly observed when a Japanese meets an acquaintance of a member of his family or when he meets a family member of one of his acquaintances. When he meets an acquaintance of his family member, he usually thanks him for his kindness to his family member, as in

Shujin (Kanai)-ga osewa-ni natte-orimasu.
主人（家内）が　おせわに　なっております。
(Thank you for your kindnesses to my husband [wife].)

And when he meets a family member of his acquaintance, he should express his gratitude to him by saying

Goshujin (Okusan)-niwa itsumo osewa-ni natte-orimasu.
(Your husband [wife] is always kind to me.)

Expressions of gratitude are regarded as more polite than compliments. Only when referring to a younger member of the listener's family can the speaker say things like

Makoto-san-wa honto-ni ii-okosan-desu-ne.
(Makoto is really a nice boy.)

without being impolite.

Referring to previous meetings

Mr. Okada called Mr. Lerner a few days ago to discuss some business. Before the business discussion he thanked him for helping his son with English the week before. And when he met Mr. Lerner this afternoon he again referred to that and thanked him. Mr. Lerner wondered if the Japanese usually repeat what they have said on the phone when they meet again in person.

*　　　*　　　*

When one meets an acquaintance after some interval, it is polite to refer to the previous meeting and express one's gratitude or apologize. For instance, when you meet someone who treated you to dinner a week before, you should thank him by saying

Senjitsu-wa gochisoosama-deshita.
先日は　ごちそうさまでした。
(Thank you for the feast the other day.)

And when you meet someone who helped you when you visited his town, you should say something like

Kyooto-dewa taihen osewa-ni narimashita.
京都では　たいへん　おせわに　なりました。
(Thank you very much for your kind help when I was in Kyoto.)

An apologetic reference is often used when you meet someone whom you talked with at a party the previous evening, as in

Yuube-wa shitsuree-shimashita.

12

(*lit.* I was rude yesterday evening.)

These expressions usually start with reference either to the time or place of the previous meeting. Common expressions used for a time reference are: *Senjitsu-wa* . . . (. . . the other day), *Kono-aida-wa* . . . (. . . the other day, less formal than *Senjitsu-wa*), *Kinoo-wa* . . . (. . . yesterday), *Yuube-wa* . . . (. . . yesterday evening), *Sakihodo-wa* . . . (. . . a while ago). The speaker usually does not specify the exact date or time as in *Sangatsu juugonichi-wa* . . . (. . . on March 15th) or *Kinoo-no sanji-wa* . . . (. . . at three o'clock yesterday afternoon).

These expressions of apology or gratitude about previous meetings can be either sincere or merely formal, but they serve to express one's concern with the other person and one's wish to reinforce good relations. Your Japanese acquaintances will usually expect you to refer to your previous meeting, and your expression of gratitude for their kindness or hospitality at that time will make them very happy. And very often, as in Mr. Okada's case mentioned above, the Japanese feel that they should express their gratitude or apologies personally even after they have mentioned them on the phone or in writing.

Parting from someone you meet every day

Mr. Lerner recently noticed that his colleagues use various expressions when they leave the office, and that *Sayonara,* which he had thought to be the most common, is actually not used very often. He wondered if he should start using *Ja* or *Osaki-ni* instead.

* * *

When one parts from one's colleagues after a day's work, such casual expressions as

Ja (So long — *lit.* Well, then)
Ja, mata (See you soon — *lit.* Well, again)

are commonly used. And when one leaves the office before others, one says

Osaki-ni (*lit.* Before you)

and the remaining workers will respond with such expressions as

Otsukaresama. (*lit.* You must be tired.)

Toward one's superiors, one says either *Shitsuree-shimasu* (Excuse me) or

Osaki-ni shitsuree-shimasu.
お先に　失礼します。
(*lit.* I'm rude enough to leave before you.)

Some people use *Sayonara* when parting from their colleagues and some do not; that depends upon how they regard their relations with each other. If they regard their fellow workers as

14

members of a very closely united group, they do not use *Sayonara*. While *Sayonara* implies the parting of two individuals, *Osaki-ni* implies a member of a group leaving the others.

This is related to the fact that *Sayonara* is never used among family members. Children use it not only to their friends but also to older people because they still do not make distinctions about whom they are talking to. When they grow up, they start using different kinds of expressions for parting depending on the listener; namely, they use *Sayonara* to their equals and *Shitsuree-shimasu* to their superiors. And when they join a group of workers, they use either *Sayonara* or other expressions toward their fellow workers.

There are various other expressions also used for parting. Some people, especially older people or women, prefer such traditional expressions as *Gokigen-yoo* (Farewell), *Gomen-kudasai(mase)* (Please excuse me), and *Gomen-nasai(mashi)* (Please excuse me). On the other hand young people, especially young women, often use *Bai-bai* (Bye).

You do not have to use many different expressions. *Sayonara* can be used when you do not have to be polite. But when politeness seems to be required, we recommend that you use *Shitsuree-shimasu* instead. And you should not use *Sayonara* to people who treat you like a family member.

Parting from family members

Mr. Lerner went to visit a town in Hokkaido, where he stayed with Miss Yoshida's relatives. When he went out for sightseeing in the morning, the wife saw him off with

Itte-rasshai.
行ってらっしゃい。
(*lit.* Please go and come back.)

Mr. Lerner responded with

Itte-mairimasu.
行ってまいります。
(*lit.* I'm going and coming back.)

While doing so, he wondered if he could also say *Sayonara.*

*　　　*　　　*

When a family member goes out, those remaining say *Itte-rasshai* and the one leaving says *Itte-kimasu* or *Itte-mairimasu.* This can never be replaced by *Sayonara.* We heard about a boy, 10 years old, who wanted a change and said *Okaasan, sayonara* when he left for school one morning. His mother frantically ran after him and asked if he was running away from home.

Family members never use *Sayonara* between themselves in any situation. When they meet outside their home and part, they say *Ja* (Well, then) or *Ja, ato-de* (Well, then, later). They use these expressions when talking on the phone too. Even when a family member is going abroad and will not be back for years, they never use *Sayonara.* In fact, family members do not use expressions that mean parting. One uses *Sayonara* to one's family members only when he is going to leave forever.

Sometimes one extends this custom toward non-family members. A neighbor may greet you with *Itte-rasshai* when you go out, and with *Okaeri-nasai* (Welcome home) when you come home.

A visitor staying with a family is usually treated as a member of that family. If he is coming back to them later, he is greeted with *Itte-rasshai* instead of *Sayonara.* Mr. Lerner was right when he responded with *Itte-mairimasu.* If he had said *Sayonara,* it would have meant that he was leaving the family for good.

When you are staying with a Japanese family and are treated like a family member, you should use family-like greetings. Even when you are leaving them after your stay, and are not likely to visit them again, it is better to use such expressions as

> *Ja, kore-de shitsuree-shimasu.*
> じゃ、これで 失礼します。
> (Well, please excuse me.)

or

> *Dewa kore-de.*
> (Well, excuse me.)

Putting an end to telephone conversations

Mr. Lerner still has difficulty ending telephone conversations. The Japanese seem to bid farewell almost endlessly; he wonders how he can successfully find a chance to say good-bye.

*   *   *

It is easy to end a telephone conversation between good friends because you can tell whether the conversation has come to an end or not, but otherwise you have to be careful about when to start saying good-bye.

The end of a telephone conversation is closed by confirming the end of the business discussion and either thanking or apologizing to the other person.

The end of a business discussion is usually confirmed by such expressions as

> *Ja, soo shimashoo-ka.*
> (Well, then, shall we do it that way?)
> *Ja, sonna tokoro-de.*
> じゃ、そんな　ところで。
> (What about doing it that way?)
> *Ja, sore-de ii-desu-ne.*
> (It's all right to do so, isn't it?)
> *Soo-yuu koto-de onegai-shimasu.*
> (Please take care of it in that way.)
> *Sore-ja, yoroshiku.*
> それじゃ、よろしく。
> (Please take care of it. Thank you.)
> *Hai, wakarimashita.*
> (Yes, I understand.)

After the confirmation, both of the speakers use expressions either of gratitude or apology. Expressions of gratitude include: *Honto-ni doomo* (Thank you indeed), *Iroiro osewa-ni narimashita* (Thank you very much for your kindnesses), *Arigatoo-gozaimashita* (Thank you very much. You've been so kind), *Tasukarimashita* (You're been so helpful). For apology, such expressions as the following are often used: *Kyoo-wa honto-ni doomo sumimasen-deshita* (I'm sorry I caused you so much trouble today), *Oyobitate-shite, sumimasen-deshita* (I'm sorry I called you up), *Ojikan-o torimashite* (Sorry I took your time). These expressions of gratitude or apology are often repeated; sometimes expressions of both kinds are used together as in *Doomo sumimasen. Arigatoo-gozaimashita.*

Then finally expressions indicating parting are used. When you don't have to be polite, you can say *Sayonara* but when you have to be polite you should say *Shitsuree-shimasu* or *Gomen-kudasai.* If you are good friends you will just say *Ja.*

This procedure is not much different from face-to-face conversation, but it seems that expressions of gratitude or apology are repeated more often in telephone conversation, and the frequency is proportionate to the degree of politeness. Therefore, we recommend that you get used to repeating similar expressions in polite telephone conversations.

Starting a business discussion

Mr. Lerner has come to be able to politely greet others and then discuss business, but he is still not at ease with starting a business discussion. He always says *Jitsu-wa* . . . when he has to start, but thinks there must be some other way. And he also wonders what he should say when the other person seems to go on talking about irrelevant matters.

* * *

You can start discussing business any time between good friends, but when you have to be polite, you must go through the appropriate steps. When people start the discussion of business after exchanging expressions of apology or gratitude about the previous meeting and talking about such topics as the weather and sports, they need a signal to show that the business discussion is going to start.

For this signal, such expressions are used as:

De, kyoo-wa nani-ka . . .
で、きょうは　なにか……
(Well, what can I do for you today? — *lit.* Then today anything . . .?)

Tokoro-de kyoo-wa . . .
By the way, what can I do for you today? — *lit.* By the way, today . . .?)

De, kyoo-wa . . .
で、きょうは……
(Well, what can I do for you today? — *lit.* Then today . . .?)

This signal is usually given by the person in a position of advantage, in terms of the business transaction. If you are meeting with someone in order to sell something or to ask for his cooperation, you are at a disadvantage, and the signal must be given by him.

After the signal is given, the other person will say

> *Jitsu-wa . . .*
> じつは……
> (As a matter of fact, . . .)

which is followed by other expressions depending on the situation, such as:

> . . . *chotto onegai-shitai koto-ga arimashite*
> (. . . I would like to ask your help.)
> . . . *chotto oshiete-itadakitai koto-ga arimashite*
> (. . . I would like to ask you about something.)
> . . . *zehi gosoodan-shitai koto-ga arimashite*
> (. . . I would like to talk with you about something.)

To be accepted as acting appropriately by Japanese businessmen, you should first decide whether you are the one who should give the signal to start the business discussion or not. If you have decided that you are not, you have to wait patiently for the other person to give the signal.

Ordering a meal at a restaurant

Mr. Lerner can usually make his wishes understood when ordering a meal at a restaurant, but he still does not know if he is saying the right thing when he wants more time to decide on his order or when he has to call a waitress to his table.

* * *

When a waiter or waitress comes to your table and asks for your order saying

Irasshaimase. Nan-ni nasaimasu-ka.
いらっしゃいませ。なんに　なさいますか。
(Welcome. What would you like to have?)

You may want more time before you decide. It is all right to say *Chotto matte-kudasai* (Please wait a moment), but usually it is enough to say

Chotto . . .

Or, when you are expecting someone, you can say

Tsure-ga kite-kara-de ii-desu-ka.
(Is it all right if I order after my friend comes?)

The waiter or waitress will come back after a while and ask you

Okimari-desu-ka.
おきまりですか。
(Have you decided?)

When you actually order, you should name the dishes and add such expressions as:

22

. . . kudasai, . . . onegai-shimasu,
. . . itadakimasu, or *. . . moraimashoo.*

There are no set Japanese expressions correspond-
ing to "What's the chef's recommendation?" You
might use such expressions as:

*Nihon-wa hajimete-nan-desu-ga, nani-ga ii-
deshoo-ne.*
(This is the first time I have visited Japan.
What do you recommend?)

*Kono omise-no hyooban-o kiite-kimashita-ga
nani-o itadaitara ii-deshoo-ne.*
(I have heard much about the good reputation
of this restaurant. What should I have?)

You may have to call the waitress' attention
when she does not come again soon after you asked
her to wait, or when you want to order something
else. Sometimes just raising your hand is sufficient, but sometimes you have to raise your voice
to call her. The Japanese word for waiter or
waitress is *kyuuji,* but this is not used for addressing one. Some people use such words as *oneesan*
(*lit.* older sister) or *ojoosan* (a young girl), but
these are not very common. The most appropriate
expression for calling them is *Sumimasen* (Excuse
me) or *Onegai-shimasu* (*lit.* I request); sometimes
both of them are used together as in *Sumimasen,
onegaishimasu.*

Visiting someone without notice

Mr. Lerner has visited the homes of Japanese acquaintances a number of times, but he still has several questions about visiting. For instance, he wonders if he can visit people without notice as many Japanese seem to do, and when he does, what expressions he should use.

*   *   *

Until some time ago, people often visited others without notice — and sometimes still do — and this set expression is used in such cases:

Chotto sono hen-made mairimashita-node . . .
(Since I happened to be in the neighborhood . . .)

The underlying idea is that one should not inform the other of one's visit and thus make him prepare for it. Actually this idea is supported by the fact that most Japanese hosts feel that they have to serve their visitors appropriate food and drink.

Nowadays calling beforehand seems to be more common, especially in big cities. As a compromise, some people call just before their visit. Since the visit will be paid on very short notice the host is not expected to make too much preparation.

When one visits someone unannounced or after short notice, it is customary to leave without going into the house. In this case, when the host says *Doozo oagari-kudasai* (Please come in), you should answer

Iie, koko-de shitsuree-shimasu.

(No, I would like to stay here — *lit.* No I will be rude enough to talk with you here.)

24

and you might add something like

> *Chotto isogimasu-node . . .*
> (I am in somewhat of a hurry.)
> *Kuruma-o matashite-imasu-node . . .*
> (A taxi is waiting for me — *lit.* I am having a
car wait for me.)

The host will not repeat his offer if he is not really
interested in having you come in. He will consent
by saying

> *Soo-desu-ka. Sore-ja . . .*
> (Is that right? In that case . . . — *lit.* Is that so?
Then . . .)

When the visitor and host have talked at the
door and their business is over, the visitor will say

> *Dewa, kore-de shitsuree-shimasu.*
> (Then, please excuse me — *lit.* Then I will be
rude enough to leave with this.)

and the host will say

> *Ocha-mo sashiagemasen-de . . .*
> (I'm sorry I didn't even offer you a cup of tea.)

If you are the visitor, you should hurriedly deny the
host's self-blame by saying
> *Iie.*

in a definite tone, and add

> *Kochira-koso totsuzen ojama-itashimashite.*
> こちらこそ　とつぜん　おじゃまいたしまして。
> (I'm sorry I came all of a sudden — *lit.* It is I
who should be blamed for being rude enough to suddenly disturb you.)

25

Giving reasons for making a request

Mr. Lerner has often noticed the Japanese around him criticizing others, especially young people, for being rude when making a request. He wonders if that is because it is difficult to make an appropriate explanation of the reason for one's request.

*   *   *

Between family members or good friends, one can explain the reason for making a request directly. For instance, one can say to his family

Kore-ja tarinai-kara moo sukoshi motte-kite.
(Because this is not enough, bring some more.)

But in social situations, one usually refrains from using *kara* because *kara,* or *dakara,* sounds as if the speaker is making the request as a matter of fact. When one tries to borrow money, it is rude to say

Okane-ga tarinai-kara kashite-kudasai.

to someone one has to be polite with. *Node* sounds less direct and is sometimes used with a more polite wording, as in

Okane-ga tarimasen-node, kashite-itadakitai-n-desu-ga.

But although this expression is polite in wording, it cannot be used when one has to sound reserved.

When making a request in a reserved way, one either politely asks a favor without directly giving the reason, or explains his needy condition and

waits for the listener to offer help. In other words, it
is more appropriate to say something like

    *Jitsu-wa yoteegai-no keehi-ga kakatte, komatte-
orimasu.*
    (As a matter of fact, I had to spend more than I
had expected, so I'm in trouble now.)

But to put the request and the reason together with
kara or *node* as in

    *Yoteegai-no keehi-ga kakatte komatte-imasu-
kara(node), okane-o okari-shitai-n-desu-ga.*

is not appropriate, because this would imply that
one is making a rightful request and has nothing to
be reserved about.
    Some people may think that it is right to ex-
plain the reason fully when making a request, but
that works only when the listener and the speaker
are on equal terms and there is no need for reserve.
    Most Japanese textbooks teach that one should
use polite words when making requests — namely,
use *kudasaimasenka* instead of *kuremasen-ka* or use
node rather than *kara*. But that only concerns the
aspect of verbal politeness. When making a request, sounding hesitant or apologetic is more important than mere verbal politeness.

Introducing oneself as someone's family member

Yesterday afternoon Mr. Lerner answered a telephone call from Mrs. Kato, the wife of one of his colleagues. She said *Osoreirimasu-ga Katoo-o onegai-shimasu* (I'm sorry to trouble you, but could you call Kato for me?). Mr. Lerner did so, but could not help wondering if it would also be appropriate for her to say *Katoo-no kanai-de gozaimasu. Shujin-o onegai-shimasu* (This is Mrs. Kato. May I speak to my husband?).

*   *   *

How to introduce one's family members or how to introduce oneself as someone's family member is determined by the situation; the question of choosing between two terms such as *kanai* and *tsuma* (wife) is not as important as whether one should use such terms at all. Usually *kanai* is considered to be more commonly used than *tsuma,* which sounds more formal, but a more important question is whether one should say *Tanaka-no kanai-desu* or *Tanaka-desu* or even say nothing at all about one's status.

When a husband has already said *Kanai-desu* to introduce his wife, she does not repeat the word *kanai* but just says *Doozo yoroshiku.* When there is nobody to introduce her and she has to introduce herself, she usually says *Tanaka-de gozaimasu* (My name is Tanaka) and the other person will say *A, Tanaka-san-no okusan-desu-ka. Doozo yoroshiku* (Oh, Mrs. Tanaka. How do you do?). Only when she wants to emphasize her being Mr. Tanaka's wife does she use the word *kanai.* The sentence *Tanaka-no kanai-desu* may sound very typical but actually this is not commonly used in daily life.

When one does not have to indicate one's relation with someone, one just gives the last name. For instance, when calling her husband's office to talk to him, a wife will say *Tanaka-o onegai-shimasu.* Giving someone's name without any term of respect is limited to family members and co-workers. Thus if someone refers to a member of a company without *san,* it is obvious that the caller is a member of the employee's family, so the recipient will call that person to the phone by saying *Tanaka-san, otaku-kara denwa-desu* (Mr. Tanaka, there's a telephone call from your home). If the recipient knows the wife personally, he may say *Tanaka-san, okusan-kara denwa-desu.* But the wife usually does not say *Tanaka-no kanai-desu* unless she is being very formal or she has some particular reason to do so. Thus it is common for a wife to say

    Tanaka-desu-ga, kyoo-wa chotto chooshi-ga warukute . . .
    (This is Tanaka; he is not feeling well.)

when reporting her husband's absence from the office.

Offering a gift

Mr. Lerner often finds it difficult to offer a gift in a polite situation. He has noticed that the Japanese seldom use expressions meaning "please accept it" or "I'd like you to accept it." Is it more polite to do without such expressions and just say *tsumaranai mono-desu-ga* and bow?

* * *

Although expressions meaning "I give you this" or "please accept it" do exist, they are not usually used when offering a gift. The appropriate method is to say something like

> *Makoto-ni tsumaranai mono-desu-ga.*
> まことに　つまらない　ものですが。
> (This is very small.)
> *Okuchi-ni awanai-kamo shiremasen-ga.*
> (*lit.* It may not suit your palate.)

by way of indicating that you are going to offer a gift.

After the listener protests by saying something like

> *Konna koto-o shite-itadaite-wa komarimasu.*
> (You shouldn't do this kind of thing.)

you should reinforce the first statement of belittling the gift as in

> *Iie, honno sukoshi-desu-kara.*
> (No, it's so small.)
> *Iie, taishita mono-ja arimasen-kara.*
> (No, it's not much.)

And when the recipient still protests, the offerer will explain the reason why he should overcome his reserve and accept it, by saying things like "It's a small token of gratitude" or "It's not enough to express my apology." Then finally the gift is received, and the recipient thanks the offerer.

This process may sound too complicated and formal, but even in familiar conversations the above-mentioned steps are often used, although the wording differs. For example,

A: *Ano, kore, tsumaranai mono-da-kedo.*
(This is very small — preliminary remark)
B: *Konna mono, moratcha warui-yo.*
(I shouldn't accept this — refusal.)
A: *Yasumono-nanda-yo.*
(It's a cheap thing — belittling the gift)
B: *Demo.*
(But — resistance)
A: *Honno kimochi-sa.*
(Just a token of my gratitude — reason why B should accept it.)
B: *Soo. Ja, sekkaku-da-kara . . . arigatoo.*
(Is that so? Then, since you insist. Thank you — acceptance)
A: *Iya.* (Not at all.)

Nowadays some Japanese, especially young people, do not use the expression *tsumaranai mono* between good friends, but belittling one's gift is always regarded as something good to do.

Asking someone to return a phone call

Mr. Lerner still finds it difficult when telephoning to leave a message for someone who is not there to call him back later. He has learned the expression . . . *to otsutae-kudasai* (please tell him . . .), but he is not sure whether he should refer to the person who is not there more politely than to the person who has answered the phone or vice versa. He often ends up choosing to call again rather than leaving a message.

*　　　*　　　*

When the person who has answered the telephone tells you that the person you want to talk to is out and asks you

Nanika okotozuke-ga oari-desu-ka.
(Would you like to leave any message?)

you can state your message. If he or she has not asked you this, you must say

Sumimasen-ga, kotozuke, onegai-dekimasu-ka.
(I'm sorry to trouble you, but could I leave a message?)

The simplest message is that you called. If you have already given your name, you should say

Denwa-ga atta-to otsutae-kudasai.
(Please tell him that I called.)

And if you haven't given your name yet, you should say

Raanaa-kara denwa-ga atta-to otsutae-kudasai.
(Please tell him that Mr. Lerner called.)

When you want the person to call you when he returns, you have to consider your relations with him or her — A — and with the person who has answered the phone — B.

I.   If you have to be polite to both A and B, you should say

Okaeri-ni nattara, denwa-o kudasaru yoo-ni otsutae-kudasai.
(Please tell him to call me when he returns.)

This is the most appropriate expression to use in such cases as calling someone at his office or calling an acquaintance at his home.

II.   If A is a good friend or family member and B is an acquaintance, you should change the first part as in

Kaettara denwa-o kureru yoo-ni otsutae-kudasai.

III.   Coversely, if A is an acquaintance and B is a good friend, change the last part, as in

Okaeri-ni nattara, denwa-o kudasaru yoo-ni mooshiagete-ne.

This is used in a case such as talking with a nurse whom you know well and asking her to give a message to the doctor, her boss.

IV.   When both A and B are good friends, you can say

Kaettara, denwa-o kureru yoo-ni itte-ne.

In all cases, you don't have to mention the name of A because it is already understood. It is more natural to simply say

Okaeri-ni nattara or *Kaettara*

than to say *Goshujin-ga okaeri-ni nattara* (when your husband returns) or *Kare-ga kaettara* (When he returns).

33

Conveying a message

Mr. Lerner sometimes answers telephone calls for his colleagues and is asked to convey a message. He can manage to do so, but he wonders if he is doing it in the right way.

* * *

It is best to start by saying that someone called while the listener was out, for example something like

Sakki Tanaka-san-kara denwa-ga arimashita.
さっき　田中さんから　電話が　ありました。
(Mr. Tanaka called you a while ago.)

As variations, you might say things like

Orusu-ni . . . (While you were out)
Sanji-goro . . . (At about three o'clock)
Sakki orusu-ni . . . (A while ago when you were out)

The order of the phrases is, first "time," next "agent," and finally "action." You can also use this pattern when referring to someone's visit, as in

Sanji-goro (orusu-ni) Tanaka-san(-to yuu kata)-ga miemashita.
((A) Mr. Tanaka came to see you at about three (while you were out).)

Then in the second sentence you should convey the message; the most common pattern is to conclude the sentence with . . . *soo-desu* (I hear, I understand), as in

Kondo-nowa taihen ki-ni itta soo-desu.

(He said that he liked the new one very much.)

Ashita-no kaigi-niwa jippun-hodo okureru soo-desu.

(He said that he would be about 10 minutes late for tomorrow's meeting.)

Instead of ... *soo-desu,* you can use a phrase meaning "he said," but saying ... *to iimashita* can sound rather childish; to be polite, you should say ... *to osshaimashita,* and in familiar conversation ... *tte* is often used as in

Ashita-no kaigi-niwa jippun-gurai okureru-tte.

The easiest way is to use two separate sentences, but you can, if you like, connect the two by using the *te* from as in

Sakki Tanaka-san-kara denwa-ga atte (more politely, *arimashite), ashita-no kaigi-niwa jippun-hodo okureru soo-desu.*

Declining an offer of help

Mr. Lerner often finds the Japanese too kind or too willing to help him. He wonders how he can appropriately decline their offers without offending them.

*　　　*　　　*

The most common phrase used to decline someone's offer is *Iie, kekkoo-desu* as in

A:　*Ocha-demo ikaga-desu-ka.* (Would you like some tea?)
B:　*Iie, kekkoo-desu. Doomo.* (No, thank you.)

You can use the same phrase when declining someone's help, too, as in

A:　*Onimotsu, omochi-shimashoo-ka.* (Can I help you with your luggage?)
B:　*Iie, kekkoo-desu. Doomo.*

Usually *kekkoo-desu* is said first and an expression of thanks comes later, but you can reverse the order as in

Arigatoo-gozaimasu. Demo kekkoo-desu.

Sometimes people decline an offer once to be polite even when they are going to accept it. In such cases, the refusal is not said with the definite tone which is used when really declining. Namely, the conversation will go something like:

A:　*Onimotsu, omochi-shimashoo.*
B:　*Iie, kekkoo-desu . . .*
A:　*Demo, omosoo-desu-yo. Doozo, doozo.*

(But it looks very heavy. Please let me help you.)

    B: *Soo-desu-ka. Doomo sumimasen.*

(Well, thank you very much.)

If B is definitely declining, he will repeat *kekkoo-desu* and make some additional comment, as in

    Iie, kekkoo-desu. Taishita nimotsu-ja arimasen-node.

(No, thank you. It's not much.)

When a Japanese acquaintance is too persistent in wanting to help you, you should dismiss his worries by convincing him that you don't need his help. For instance, when your acquaintance insists on going with you even though you think you can go alone, you should use such expressions as *nantoka ... dekiru* (be able to manage somehow) as in

    Nantoka hitori-de ikemasu-kara.

(I can manage to go by myself.)

Sometimes you can express a certain wish so that he will give up his offers, as in

    Nihongo-o tsukatte-mitai-node.

(I'd like to try out my Japanese.)

    Chotto booken-shite-mitai-node.

(I'd like to have an adventure.)

And it is a good idea to add something like

    Tochuu-de wakaranaku nattara denwa-shimasu-kara.

(I'll call you if I get lost.)

or

    Dekinaku nattara, tasukete-kudasai.

(Please help me if I find it impossible.)

Expressing gratitude for help

Mr. Lerner expresses his gratitude by saying *Arigatoo-gozaimasu* when he is offered or has received help, but he wonders if there are more appropriate expressions he should be using instead.

*   *   *

To accept someone's offer of help, one should say

Sumimasen. Ja, onegai-shimasu.

or

Arigatoo-gozaimasu. Ja, onegai-shimasu.

To be more polite, *Mooshiwake arimasen* or *Osoreirimasu* is used in place of *Sumimasen* or *Arigatoo-gozaimasu,* and *onegai-itashimasu* for *onegai-shimasu.* Between good friends, men usually say *Warui-ne. Ja, tanomu-yo* and women *Warui-wane. Ja, onegai-suru-wa.*

After some help has been received, one usually says

Arigatoo-gozaimashita.
ありがとうございました。

While *Arigatoo-gozaimasu* is used before the action of helping starts or during its performance, *Arigatoo-gozaimashita* is used when the action has been completed. This implies that the action of helping has been completed after a long time or with much effort.

In a similar way, the *ta* form is also used for apology when the speaker wants to emphasize that an action has finally been completed. For instance, one uses *Sumimasen* when one feels that he is going to cause someone trouble or that he actually is causing someone trouble, but when that is finished, one says

> *Doomo sumimasen-deshita.*
> どうも　すみませんでした。

or

> *Honto-ni sumimasen-deshita.*

meaning "I'm so sorry that you have been caused so much trouble." More politely, one can say

> *Makoto-ni mooshiwake arimasen-deshita.*

In familiar conversations *Warukatta-ne* or *Warukatta-wane* is used.

After thanking someone for his help, one often indicates that it has been valuable by saying things like

> *Okagesama-de, hayaku katazukimashita.*
> (Thanks to your help, I could finish it quickly.)
> *Okagesama-de ii mono-ga dekimashita.*
> (Thanks to your help, I could make a good one.)
> *Tetsudatte-itadaite, honto-ni tasukarimashita.*
> (Your help has saved me so much trouble.)

Making explanations

Mr. Lerner feels that it is rather difficult to make explanations in social situations. Explanations should be sufficient and yet not overdone, but he has the unpleasant memory of having once said *Shitte-imasu-ka* (Do you know?) to Mr. Mori, the director of the company, in trying to find out whether he should give more of an explanation or not.

* * *

It is impolite to give more explanation than necessary because it implies that one thinks the listener is ignorant. But checking the extent of someone's knowledge is difficult when one has to be polite. This is especially true when the explanation concerns a field the listener feels he knows. Asking with direct expressions such as

> *Shitte-imasu-ka.* (Do you know?)
> *Gozonji-desu-ka.* (Do you know? — more polite)

is also impolite when it concerns the listener's intelligence or professional knowledge.

It is ideal for the speaker to know the listener well enough to be able to give the exact amount of information needed without checking his knowledge. This was probably possible when people lived in a small society and shared the same knowledge, but it is impossible between two people who do not know each other very well. Therefore one has to guess the scope of knowledge of the listener to a certain extent and supplement this with linguistic devices.

To avoid sounding impolite, one device is to use phrases meaning "as you know." There are several expression like this in common use, such as *gozonji-kamo shiremasen-ga* (you may know this already but), *gozonji-to omoimasu-ga* (I think you know it already but), *gozonji-no yoo-ni* (as you know), *goshoochi-no yoo-ni* (as you know), *goannai-no toori* (as you are familiar with), and so on. For example, one may say something like

Kachoo-wa moo gozonji-kamo shiremasen-ga, konna kikai-ga deta-n-desu-ga . . .
(to a section chief — You may know this already, but this new machine has come out.)

If the section chief says that he knows about it, one stops explaining. If the section chief says something like

Iya, shiranai-ne. Donnano?
(No, I don't know. What is it like?)

one can go ahead and explain further.

Responding to a compliment

Like many other foreigners living in Japan, Mr. Lerner is often complimented on his Japanese. He usually answers *Iie, sonna koto-wa arimaseri* (No, that isn't so), but he wonders if there are more appropriate expressions he could use.

*   *   *

How to respond to a compliment depends on the situation and the purpose of the compliment. Very often a compliment is said as a kind of conversation opener. For instance, a conversation between a host and visitor may start as follows:

Host: *Doozo kochira-e.* (This way, please.)
Visitor: *Shitsuree-shimasu. Ii osumai-desu-ne.* (Thank you. You have a very nice house.)
Host: *Iie. Maa doozo oraku-ni.*
(Thanks — *lit.* No. Please make yourself at home.)

The host will dismiss the compliment lightly, but if the visitor shows that he is really interested in the house, the host will start admitting its good points.

A compliment on your Japanese is very often said as a kind of opening remark toward a foreigner because many Japanese, not being used to talking with foreigners, feel that they have to say something of this nature to start the conversation. In such cases, you can simply answer *Iie, sonna koto-wa arimasen* or *Iie, sorehodo-demo arimasen.* (No. I'm not so good.) When the speaker is really admiring your Japanese and is interested in it, he will repeat the compliment and then you should act differently.

(1)   One reaction is to accept it happily as in

Soo-desu-ka. Doomo arigatoo.
(Do you think so? Thank you very much.)
and add
Hayaku motto joozu-ni naritai-to omotte-imasu.
(I want to become better as soon as possible.)

(2)   Another reaction is to admit the compliment to a certain degree and say something like

Madamada heta-desu-ga, mae-yori sukoshi yoku natta-kamo shiremasen.
(I'm still poor, but I may have improved a little.)

(3)   Another is to admit the improvement and attribute it to someone else as in

Minasan-no okage-desu.
(That's because everybody has helped me.)
Sensee-ga ii-kara-desu.
(That's because I have a good teacher.)

You can combine (1) and (3) as in

Soo-desu-ka. Doomo. Minasan-no okage-desu.
そうですか。どうも。みなさんの　おかげです。

One has to choose the most appropriate way depending on the situation and your relations with the speaker. Between good friends you can readily admit your competence, and flatly denying it can be improper when you have just proved it. But generally speaking, it is recommended that you deny the compliment first, and when necessary, partially admit it and attribute it to someone else.

Describing physical problems — stomachache

Yesterday morning Mr. Lerner had a stomachache and went to see a doctor. When the doctor asked him what the matter was, he answered

Onaka-ga itai-desu.
(I have a stomachache.)

The doctor then asked *Dono hen-desu-ka* (What part?), and while pressing there with his hand, asked *Donna fuu-ni itamimasu-ka.* (What kind of pain do you have?) Mr. Lerner said simply *Hidoku itamimasu* (Terribly painful), but the doctor seemed to want a more concrete description; he asked

Kirikiri-desu-ka, shikushiku-desu-ka.
きりきりですか、しくしくですか。

*   *   *

Kirikiri itamu means that you feel as if a nail were being driven into the body; it can describe a sharp pain not only in the stomach or intestines but also in the heart, head or various other parts of the body.

On the other hand, *shikushiku itamu* is used when one has a pain in one's stomach or intestines which is not very sharp but is felt continuously for some time. This word is also used to describe a person, usually a woman or child, continuing to weep quietly.

Another important fact about a pain is whether it is felt with or without stimulus from outside. You can explain this by such expressions as

Tsuyoku osu-to itamimasu.
(I feel pain when it is pressed hard.)
Chotto oshita-dake-de itamimasu.
(I feel pain when it is lightly pressed.)
Nanimo shinakute-mo itamimasu.
(I feel pain when nothing has been done.)

It is also necessary to tell the doctor whether the trouble is felt when you are hungry or full; this can be described as

Onaka-ga suku-to itamimasu.
(I feel pain when I am hungry.)
Shokuji-no ato itamimasu.
(I feel pain after meals.)
Furai-nado-o taberu-to mune-ga yakemasu.
(I feel heartburn when I have fried food.)

And the doctor will also be interested in when the trouble started and whether it has been constant or not. You can explain this as

Kinoo-no yuugata itamidashite, zuutto tsuzuite-imasu.
(The pain started yesterday evening and has been going on ever since.)
Yuube-kara tokidoki itamimasu.
(It has been hurting off and on since last night.)

Describing physical troubles — headache

A few days ago Mr. Lerner suffered from a headache, probably because of fatigue. When Miss Yoshida at the office told him that he looked like he was in a bad mood, he answered

Atama-ga itai-n-desu. (I have a headache.)

Miss Yoshida asked if the pain was bad, so he answered that his head was throbbing. Then she said

Aa, zukizuki itamu-n-desu-ne.　ずきずき
*　　*　　*

There are several expressions used to describe headaches. *Kirikiri,* which is often used for sharp pains in the stomach, can be used for headaches, too. *Zukizuki* refers to pain that occurs regularly like a pulse; it corresponds to the English "throbbing pain." It is used for pain in various parts of the body, especially with headaches and wounds.

Sometimes *"n"* is added as in

Zukinzukin itamimasu.　ずきんずきん

which describes a very strong pain. The *"n"* sound is used to emphasize the impact of some repeated action. For instance, *doshidoshi aruku* means "to walk thudding along," and saying *doshindoshin aruku* emphasizes the heaviness of the movement. You might put it as

doshi doshi
doshin! doshin!

When you feel as if your head is covered with a helmet and the helmet is being beaten with a hammer, you should say

Atama-ga gangan suru. がんがん

Gangan refers to a clamorous noise.

Besides pain, we often have other troubles with our head. After a sleepless night we may feel that it is not working well. This condition is described as

Yoku nemurenakatta-node, atama-ga omoi-desu.
(I couldn't sleep well, so my head is not working well — *lit.* . . . my head is heavy.)

Or, you may sometimes feel that your head is still sleeping.

Okita bakari-de atama-ga hakkiri shimasen.
(I have just woken up and my head is not clear yet — *lit.* . . . my head is hazy.)

You can replace *okita bakari-de* by *jetto-ragu-de* (because of jet lag.)

Headaches can also be used figuratively to refer to what psychologically bothers you. For example, two people may talk as follows:

A: *Ano mondai, kaiketsu-shimashita-ka.*
(Was that problem solved?)
B: *Iie, mada-na-n-desu. Atama-ga itai-desu-yo.*
(Not yet. It's really a headache.)

The expression *atama-ga itai* is often replaced by *zutsuu-ga suru,* which sounds slightly more formal.

Describing physical problems — being hurt in a fall

Yesterday morning Mr. Lerner stumbled on the stairs at the railway station when he tried to dodge an old Japanese woman who hurriedly pushed by him. He seemed to have hit his left elbow, which hurt a little during the day. When he unconsciously touched it and frowned, Miss Yoshida asked him what the matter was. He answered

Kesa eki-de taoremashita.

meaning "I fell at the station this morning." She looked very concerned, and he had to explain more fully.

* * *

The word *taoreru* refers to someone or something falling flatly as in:

Taifuu-de ki-ga nanbon-mo taoremashita.
(Many trees fell down in the typhoon.)
Nagurarete aomuke-ni taoremashita.
(He was hit and fell on his head.)

It also figuratively refers to a person collapsing because of serious illness or fatigue. Whether physically or figuratively, referring to a person using *taoreru* implies a serious condition; therefore Miss Yoshida looked concerned when Mr. Lerner said *taoremashita.*

Mr. Lerner should have used the verb *korobu*, which means "to stumble and fall," as in

Koronde hiji-o uchimashita.
ころんで　ひじを　打ちました。
(I fell and hit my elbow.)

48

Koronde utta tokoro-ga itamimasu.
(The place I hit when I fell hurts.)

When you have fallen, you may have serious pain and have to go to a doctor. The following expressions will help you explain your condition:

Ugokasu-to itamimasu.
(I feel pain when I move it.)
Harete zukizuki itamimasu.
(It has swollen and I feel throbbing pain.)
Surimuita tokoro-ga hirihiri itamimasu.
(The place where the skin was scraped smarts.)

Honno — Signaling devaluation

The other day Mr. Takada offered Mr. Lerner a gift for helping him with his English. Mr. Lerner said that he had never expected that and did not want to take it. Then Mr. Takada said

Honno kimochi-da-kara . . .
ほんの　気持ちだから……
(*lit.* Since it is merely my feeling.)

Mr. Lerner understood that this was a set expression urging him to accept it, but wondered how *honno* (merely, only) can modify *kimochi* (feeling).

*　　　*　　　*

The word *honno* is used to signal that what comes next is regarded as small by the speaker. This is similar to the English "only" or "merely" as in

Eki-kara chikai-desu. Aruite honno gofun-gurai-desu.
(It's near the station. Only a five-minute walk.)
Honno sukoshi-de kekkoo-desu.
(Please give me just a little bit of it; Just a little bit will do.)

It is also used when the modified words do not indicate number or quantity.

Mada honno kodomo-desu.
(He's only a child.)
Honno joodan-desu-yo.
(It's only a joke.)

Since this word has a devaluating implication,

it is often used in expressing modesty, as in

Naratta-to itte-mo honno shoho-desu.
(It's true I've studied it, but just the first step.)
Honno tsumaranai mono-desu-ga . . .
(This is a very small thing, (but please accept it).)

A: *Senjitsu-wa taihen gochisoosama-deshita.*
(Thank you very much for the nice meal the other day.)
B: *Iie, honno ariawase-de.*
(Not at all. We just served you what we happened to have.)

When offering a gift, *honno kimochi-desu* is often said to devaluate it and urge the other person to accept it. The underlying idea is this: the amount of a gift should be proportionate to the degree of gratitude, but this gift is too small to express my gratitude. Therefore this is merely a token of my feeling of thanks and not of the appropriate monetary value.

Tazunete-kuru — Describing actions directed at the speaker

Yesterday morning Mr. Lerner complimented Miss Yoshida on her new necklace. She thanked him and said

Kyuushuu-no ane-ga okutte-kita-n-desu.
九州の　姉が　送ってきたんです。
(My sister in Kyushu sent it to me.)

Mr. Lerner wondered if *okutte-kureta* can be used with the same meaning. He learned this expression . . . *te-kuru* once, but has not used it very often.

*　　*　　*

The verb *kuru* added to the *te* form of other verbs is used, among other usages, to indicate that someone's action is directed toward the speaker. In other words . . . *te-kuru* in this usage means "to me," and consequently *watashi-ni* is not necessary when . . . *te-kuru* is used. For example it is more appropriate to say

Yamamoto-san-ga kore-o okutte-kimashita.
(Mr. Yamamoto sent this to me.)
than
Yamamoto-san-ga watashi-ni kore-o okurimashita.

Similarly,
Yamamoto-san-ga yuube tazunete-kimashita
(Mr. Yamamoto came to see me yesterday evening.)

is usually used rather than

. . . *ga watashi-o tazunemashita.*

Kureru or *kudasaru* (humble) also indicate that someone's action is directed toward the speaker, as in

Ane-ga kore-o okutte-kuremashita.
(My sister sent this to me.)
Sensee-ga oshiete-kudasaimashita.
(My teacher taught me this.)

The difference between . . . *te-kuru* and . . . *te-kureru* is that the latter implies the speaker's gratitude while the former simply indicates the direction of the action. Thus, one may say

Ano-hito, mata mendoona koto-o tanonde-kimashita.
(He made a troublesome request of me again.)

but . . . *te-kureru* is not usually said in this situation.

And these expressions are also used in place of *anata-ni* or *anata-o* when the speaker talks from the viewpoint of the listener, as in

Yamada-san yuube denwa-shite-kimashita-ka.
(Did Mr. Yamada call you yesterday evening?)

. . . *te-kureru* can also be used in this way but it is more complicated because it is difficult to put yourself in the listener's place when gratitude is involved.

Hito-ni osareru — Suffering from someone's actions

When Mr. Lerner arrived at the office one day, Miss Yoshida noticed that the back of his coat was soiled. While taking it off, Mr. Lerner said

Dareka-ga densha-no naka-de yogoshita-n-deshoo.
(I think someone dirtied it on the train.)

Miss Yoshida then said

Watashi-mo fuku-o yogosareta koto-ga arimasu.
(I've had my clothes dirtied too.)

Mr. Lerner wondered if he should have used the passive form as she did.

* * *

When someone's actions have caused damage or been a nuisance to the speaker, it is common to use the . . . *areru* form of the verb as in

Hito-ni jirojiro miraremashita.
(I was stared at by others.)
Doroboo-ni saifu-o toraremashita.
(I had my wallet stolen by a robber.)

It is possible to describe someone's action without using the passive form, as in

Hito-ga watashi-o jirojiro mimashita.
(People stared at me.)
Doroboo-ga watashi-no saifu-o torimashita.
(A robber stole my wallet).

These two sentences describe the facts as if they

had nothing to do with the speaker's feelings. In cases when someone's action has definitely caused damage or been a nuisance, it is more appropriate to use the passive form. In fact, the latter two sentences sound as if they were examples in grammar books and unnatural.

The same fact, needless to say, is taken differently depending on the speaker. When the family next door has had a noisy party, for instance, one person will say

> *Tonari-de paatii-o yatta-node urusakatta.*
> となりで　パーティを　やったので　うるさかった。

while another person may say

> *Tonari-de paatii-o yarareta-node, urusakatta.*
> となりで　パーティを　やられたので　うるさかった。

The latter reflects the speaker's displeasure more directly. It is true that whether to use the passive or not is a matter of choice, but in cases where the speaker is expected to feel annoyed, the passive form is regarded as appropriate and not using it will sound strange.

Migi-ni magarimasu — Giving directions

Yesterday afternoon when Mr. Lerner was walking along the street with Miss Yoshida, an old woman asked them how to go to the nearest railway station. Miss Yoshida pointed to the street corner and started giving directions, saying

> *Ano kado-made ittara, migi-ni magarimasu. . . .*
> あの　角まで　行ったら　右に　まがります……
> (Go to that corner, turn to the right. . . .)

Mr. Lerner noticed that all her sentences ended in . . . *masu.* He wondered if that was different from using *kudasai,* as in *Migi-ni magatte-kudasai.*

*　　　*　　　*

The . . . *masu* form is used for giving directions as well as . . . *te-kudasai.* The difference between the two is that . . . *te-kudasai* is said, either as a request or command, directly to the listener while the . . . *masu* form is not directed to the listener.

The . . . *te-kudasai* form used for giving directions implies that the speaker is taking the leadership and has confidence in the matter. For instance, doctors and nurses often use this form with their patients as in

> *Kono kusuri-wa ichinichi sankai, shokugo-ni nonde-kudasai.*
> (Please take this medicine three times a day after meals.)
> *Tabesuginai yoo-ni shite-kudasai.*
> (Please try not to overeat.)

On the other hand the . . . *masu* form is used when the speaker wants to give the impression that he is explaining something for the listener's information rather than directly urging him to follow his directions. The ... *masu* form, when used in explanation, sounds more impersonal and detached than the ... *te-kudasai* form. Therefore it is used more often in polite situations. For instance, when professional cooks give instruction in cooking on TV, they can choose to use either the ... *te-kudasai* form or ... *masu.* Generally speaking, they tend to use the ... *masu* form, as in

Hajime-ni shio-to koshoo-o furimasu.
(First, sprinkle on salt and pepper.)
Abura-no ondo-wa takaku shimasu.
(Raise the temperature of the oil very high.)

If Miss Yoshida had said *Migi-ni magatte-kudasai* when she was telling the old woman how to go to the station, she would have sounded too direct or condescending; the *kudasai* form would be appropriate if she were telling a taxi driver how to take her somewhere.

Doo sureba yoroshii-deshoo—Asking for instructions

When Mr. Lerner was talking with Mr. Mori, the director of the company, Miss Yoshida came in and asked Mr. Mori for instructions about how to type a part of his letter. She said

Koko-wa doo uteba yoroshii-deshoo.
(How should I type this?)

and Mr. Mori answered, while writing it out on a piece of paper

Koo-yuu fuu-ni utte-kureru-to ii-gane.
(Would you type it this way?)

While listening to this exchange, Mr. Lerner wondered if he had been using the right expressions when asking for directions; he usually said ... *shinakereba narimasen-ka* (Must I . . .?)

*   *   *

Using ... *nakereba narimasen-ka,* as in *Doo utanakereba narimasen-ka,* can be understood, but it is not common in social situations. Answering a question with this form, as in *Koo utanakereba narimasen,* is also uncommon in actual life; it is classroom Japanese.

Among several expressions used for asking for instructions, *doo sureba ii-deshoo* (more politely, ... *yoroshii-deshoo*) sounds the most humble because it implies that the speaker is interested in knowing what is the right way to do something. For instance, when you come across a kanji compound you do not know how to read, it is most appropriate to say

Kore-wa doo yomeba ii-deshoo.
これは　どう　読めば　いいでしょう。
(How should I read this?)

The . . . *sureba ii-deshoo* form is also used when asking someone's wishes politely, as in

Doko-e ukagaeba yoroshii-deshoo.
(Where would you like me to come?)
Nanji-ni omochi-sureba yoroshii-deshoo.
(When would you like me to bring it?)

To mean "How should I do this?", the following expressions should be avoided in social situations because they sound like classroom speech.

Doo shinakereba narimasen-ka.
Doo suru-beki-desu-ka.
Yomikata-wa nan-desu-ka.

Saying *Doo shimasu-ka* is all right and *Doo suru-n-desu-ka* is also acceptable, but these are not as humble as *Doo sureba ii-deshoo.*

Arakajime yoyaku-suru —
Redundancy

When Mr. Lerner and his colleagues were discussing plans for an outing, someone said that they should make reservations at the restaurant where they were planning to have lunch. Miss Yoshida agreed and said

Soo-desu-ne. Arakajime yoyaku-shita hoo-ga anzen-desu-ne.
(That's right. It's safer to make reservations beforehand.)

Mr. Lerner agreed, but at the same time he wondered if her sentence wasn't redundant in saying *arakajime yoyaku-suru.*

*　　　*　　　*

The word *yoyaku* itself means "making a promise beforehand"; the kanji used for *yo* in this word means "beforehand," as also seen in such compounds as *yohoo* (forecast), *yoshuu* (preparatory study), and *yokoku* (previous notice). Therefore it is correct to say that *arakajime yoyaku-suru* is redundant.

But using two words of similar meaning together is rather common in spoken Japanese. Take, for example, the sentence *Ashita-no ban gogo kuji-goro denwa-shimasu* (I will telephone you at about 9 tomorrow night). When this sentence is written down and one looks at it carefully and critically, one may notice that *ban* and *gogo* are redundant and that one could say *Ashita-no ban kuji-goro* or *Ashita-no gogo kuji-goro* instead. But when used in conversation, this type of redundancy is usually not noticed, and people often find it helpful for making understanding easier since when one hears as far as *Ashita-no ban* (tomorrow night), he has a rough idea of a certain time, and when he next hears *gogo kuji-goro* (around 9 p.m.), he defines this time more precisely.

Going back to *arakajime yoyaku-suru,* this is also natural and easy to understand, because by hearing *arakajime,* the listener mentally prepares for doing something beforehand, and then by hearing *yoyaku,* he pins the idea down.

Otsukaresama used as an expression of meeting and parting

Mr. Lerner and his colleagues went on an overnight trip together last weekend. When they arrived at the small *minshuku* (non-professional inn), the owner and a few employees stood at the entrance and greeted them with

Irasshaimase. Otsukaresama-deshita.
いらっしゃいませ。おつかれさまでした。
(Welcome. You must be tired.)

This greeting seemed pleasing to his colleagues, but Mr. Lerner wondered why *Otsukaresama,* an expression of sympathy for other people's labor, was used to welcome guests.

*   *   *

The expression *Otsukaresama* is used when meeting someone who has finished working or who has gone through some hardship. A wife will greet her husband with this, and office workers also will use this when another worker at the office comes back from a business trip.

At railway stations and on trains, passengers are often comforted with *Otsukaresama* because riding in trains is a tiring business. Thus at the destination of a train or bus, passengers are often told

Otsukaresama-deshita.   Maido   gojoosha arigatoo-gozaimasu.
(You must be tired. Thank you for riding our train/bus.)

Employees at inns will also greet their guests with *Otsukaresama* because they must have ridden in trains or cars and become tired before arriving.

A similar expression of appreciation for other people's labor is *Gokuroosama*. This is also said to someone who has worked hard. The difference between *Gokuroosama* and *Otsukaresama* is that the former implies that the speaker appreciates the listener having performed his duty. Therefore an announcer at a railway station can say *Gokuroosama* to commuters coming home from work in the evening, but he can't use it to passengers who have gone on a pleasure trip. Some people avoid using *Gokuroosama* as an expression of appreciation toward others because they do not want to sound as if they were judging whether the listener had worked hard as a duty or not; they prefer saying *Otsukaresama* or *Osewasama* even to someone who has worked for them.

Otsukaresama is often used among co-workers when they part after the day's work is finished; like *Ja* or *Ja, mata,* this is used in place of *Sayoonara* among co-workers. Sometimes older people only say *Otsukaresama* and younger ones *Otsukaresama-deshita* or — *de-gozaimashita* which sounds more polite.

Endoo or *Endoo-mame* — Changes in the meaning of words

Mr. Lerner was having dinner at the Takadas' last Saturday evening. When he asked what the Japanese name for "green peas" was, Mrs. Takada said

Endoo-mame-desho?
(That's *endoo-mame,* isn't it?)

Then Mr. Takada said it should be just

Endoo.

because the *doo* of *endoo* means "peas." Then they consulted several dictionaries and found that some of them give just *endoo* and some say that *endoo-mame* means "peas of the plant called *endoo.*" Thus it seemed there was no conclusion as to which was right as the Japanese name of "green peas."

*   *   *

As Mr. Takada pointed out, the *doo* of *endoo* stands for "peas"; it is the same kanji as the *too* of *toofu,* but it has undergone phonetic change and become *doo.* If you write *endoo-mame* in kanji, therefore, the same kanji is used twice. 豌豆豆 Since the kanji *en* has "pea" as its radical, actually *endoomame* has three "peas" when written in kanji. These days, the word *endoo* is usually written in *hiragana* or *katakana,* and people seldom think of the kanji when saying the word. People have forgotten that *doo* stands for "peas" and say *endoomame,* especially when distinguishing the peas from the plant.

Another example of forgetting the original kanji is *bakuchi-uchi* 博打打ち (gambler). The word *bakuchi* originally was *baku-uchi* (gambling, gambler); *baku-uchi* was then shortened to *bakuchi* and *uchi* (playing, player) added later. Thus the word *bakuchi-uchi* is redundant, but most people are not conscious of this, not knowing the etymology. But when they look at this word written in kanji and see that the same kanji is used twice, they start suspecting that something is wrong. (This word also is usually written in *hiragana* now.)

Although the Japanese do not pay much attention to the original meaning of words when speaking, once they start discussing them they start thinking about the kanji used for writing them. It seems they do not speak in kanji but often think in kanji, even after the number of kanji used in daily life has been decreased.

Saremasu-ka—Expression of respect

When Mr. Lerner had some beer with Mr. Okada and his colleagues the other day, one of them asked him

Supootsu-wa nanika saremasu-ka.
(Do you do any sports?)

Mr. Lerner had to think about the expression *saremasu-ka* for a moment before he realized that it was another polite form of *suru*. He wondered if this was different from *nasaru* or *oyari-ni naru.*

*　　　*　　　*

The . . . *areru* form of verbs is used to show respect as well as to indicate the passive voice. *Sareru* means either "to do" (polite) or "to be done"; *oshieraremashita* can be either "he taught" (polite) or "I was taught."

Using the . . . *areru* form for showing respect is, however, rather limited in usage. It is most often used in official announcements or public speech, where personal feelings are not usually expressed. For instance, a master of ceremonies will often use this form when introducing the speaker to the audience, as in

Yamamoto-sensee-wa kono tabi Chuugoku-yori kaeraremashite . . .
(Prof. Yamamoto has recently returned from China and . . .)

And a newspaper reporter will often use this when addressing a VIP, as in

Daijin-wa kore-ni tsuite doo omowaremasu-ka.

(What do you think about this, Mr. Minister?)

When speaking on a personal level, other expressions of respect such as *okaeri-ni naru* and *omoi-ni naru* are used more often than the . . . *areru* form; this is especially true with women.

This form is often used together with kanji compounds which sound formal, as in

Yamamoto-sensee-wa kono tabi Chuugoku-yori kikoku-saremashite . . .

山本先生は　この　たび　中国より　帰国されまして……

(Prof. Yamamoto has recently returned from China and . . .)

Daijin-wa kono mondai-ni doo taisho-saremasu-ka.

(How are you going to deal with this problem, Mr. Minister?)

The . . . *areru* form is sometimes used in personal conversations, too, especially by men, when the speaker thinks he should sound reserved. Mr. Okada's colleague must have used this form with Mr. Lerner because he felt he should sound formal since he had just met him.

Soryaa . . . — An indication of one's opinion

Yesterday afternoon several people were listening to Mr. Takada explain his proposed project at the office, when Mr. Kato, one of his colleagues, said

> *Soryaa . . .* そりゃあ……
> (*lit.* That . . .)

Mr. Lerner thought this was too short to indicate what Mr. Kato meant, but everyone seemed to understand that Mr. Kato was critical of the project. Mr. Lerner wondered how such a short phrase can be sufficient to indicate one's opinion.

* * *

Sorya is a contraction of *sore-wa;* in the same way, *kore-wa* becomes *korya* and *are-wa, arya* in familiar conversation. When the speaker uses a dangling tone, the *"a"* sound is prolonged as in *soryaa . . .*

Sore-wa can be followed by various phrases. When one wants to agree, it is usually followed by a phrase indicating approval as in

> *Sore-wa soo-desu.* (That's right.)
> *Sore-wa ii-desu-ne.* (That's good.)

Or, when one's definitely disagreeing, he will say

> *Sore-wa dame-da.* (That won't do.)
> *Sore-wa hantai-desu.* (I'm opposed to that.)

When the speaker wants to express a negative judgment, the sentence often includes *ga* or *keredomo* as in

Sore-wa soo-desu-ga, chotto mondai-ga arimasu-ne.

(That's right, but there's a problem with it.)

Sore-wa soo-kamo shiremasen-keredomo, watashi-wa sansee-shikanemasu.

(You may be right, but I can't agree with you.)

And when the speaker is reserved, the negative phrase after *ga* or *keredomo* is often left out as in

Sore-wa soo-desu-ga . . .
Sore-wa soo-kamo shiremasen-keredomo . . .

Sometimes even the first phrase, *Sore-wa,* is sufficient to indicate the speaker's negative judgment. For this purpose *Sore-wa* or *Sorya* is pronounced with a dangling tone as in *Soryaa . . .* On the other hand, when the speaker is positively agreeing or is definite about his opinion, *Sorya* is started with a high pitch and falls sharply.

Thus everybody understood that Mr. Kato was disagreeing by just listening to his *Soryaa . . .*, which was said with a dangling tone. The difference in the tone makes the intention of the speaker clear.

... te-imasen used to indicate incompletion

Yesterday afternoon when Mr. Lerner and his colleagues were having tea together, someone referred to a best seller written by a famous baseball player, and many of them said that they had read it, but Miss Yoshida said

Mada yonde-imasen. まだ　読んでいません。

Mr. Lerner wondered if it is also correct to say *Yomimasen-deshita* in this case.

*　　　*　　　*

The *... mashita* form is used to indicate that you have completed an action, as in

Moo yomimashita. (I have read it.)
Yomiowarimashita. (I have finished reading it.)

But to indicate that you haven't completed an action, you should use the *... te-imasen* form instead of *... masen-deshita.* At lunch time, for example, when asked if you have had lunch already, you should say either

Moo tabemashita (I have had it.)

or

Mada tabete-imasen. (I haven't had it yet.)
(You can also simply say *Mada-desu.*)

It is wrong to say *Tabemasen-deshita,* which should be used when you are referring to a specific time in the past as in

Kinoo-wa isogashikatta-node hirugohan-o tabemasen-deshita.

(I was so busy that I didn't have lunch yesterday.)

Or, when a question concerns a specific time, as in

Yuube-no shichiji-no nyuusu, mimashita?
(Did you watch the TV news at 7 yesterday evening?)

you can say *Iie, mimasen-deshita.* (No, I didn't watch it.)
In the same way, to a question often asked by your Japanese acquaintances,

Nihon-no seekatsu-ni naremashita-ka.
(Have you gotten used to living in Japan?)

you should answer either

Ee, daibu/sukoshi naremashita.
(Yes, I have gotten quite/a little used to it.)
or
Iie, mada narete-imasen.
(No, I haven't gotten used to it.)

It is wrong to say *Iie, naremasen-deshita,* because you are referring to a present condition rather than a certain time in the past.

71

... *te* form used to indicate a reason

When Mr. Lerner met Miss Yoshida on Monday morning, she asked him if he had gone to see the chrysanthemum exhibition near his house. He answered

Ame-ga futte ikimasen-deshita.
(It being rainy, I didn't go.)

Miss Yoshida understood but she mumbled to herself *ikemasen-deshita-deshoo?*

*　　　*　　　*

Phrases ending in the ... *te* form of a verb or adjective are used in various way. One usage is to indicate a reason, as in

Jikan-ga nakute, yomemasen-deshita.
時間が　なくて、読めませんでした。
(Having no time, I couldn't read it.)
Shigoto-ga takusan atte, terebi-mo mirarenai.
(Being busy, I can't even watch TV.)

When the *te* form is used in this way to indicate a reason, the phrases preceding and following the *te* form must belong to the same category; namely, if the phrase preceding the *te* form concerns something that the speaker cannot control, the phrase following it must also concern what cannot be controlled by the speaker. Therefore, if the phrase ending in the *te* form indicates that some unavoidable situation such as rainfall has inconvenienced you, you should use ... *emasen* or ... *dekimasen,* which refer to what you cannot control with your will. Therefore, instead of *ikimasen-*

72

deshita, Mr. Lerner should have used such phrases as

> *ikemasen-deshita* (I couldn't go)
> *dame-deshita* (I couldn't do so)
> *muri-deshita* (it was impossible)

It is not appropriate to say *ikimasen-deshita* because it indicates the speaker's will.

In the same way, a phrase like

> *Okane-ga nakute* . . . (Having no money)

is usually followed by such phrases as

> *kaemasen* (I can't buy it)
> *haraemasen* (I can't pay).

It is not appropriate to say *kaimasen* (I will not buy it) or *haraimasen* (I will not pay).

On the other hand, if you use *node* or *kara* to indicate the reason, you do not have to follow this rule. Namely, you can say either

> *Okane-ga nai-node kaemasen.*
> (Because I don't have the money for it, I cannot buy it.)

or

> *Okane-ga nai-node kaimasen.*
> (Because I don't have the money for it, I will not buy it.)

... *ta* used to indicate the completion of an action

Miss Yoshida told Mr. Lerner that her father likes to wear kimono when he relaxes, so Mr. Lerner asked

Mainichi kaisha-kara kaeru toki, kimasu-ka.
(Does he wear one every day when he returns from his office?)

Miss Yoshida laughed and said *Ee*. Mr. Lerner was not sure what he had said wrong.

*   *   *

Such verbs as *kaeru* (go home), *kuru* (come), *modoru* (return) and *tsuku* (arrive) are used to refer to movement. When they are used in the present tense, they refer only to the process of moving, not to the completion of the motion. Thus, when you say

uchi-e kaeru toki,

you are referring to a person who is moving toward his house. *Uchi-e kaeru toki kimono-o kimasu* sounds as if someone takes a kimono out of his locker when work is over and wears it home. One may imagine a railway station during the evening rush hour filled with businessmen in *yukata*. You have to say

uchi-e kaetta toki

to mean "when he is home," regardless of the tense. You can think of this as meaning when he has finished the action of returning and is home.

It is perfectly grammatical in Japanese to say things like

74

Ashita hayaku kita hito-ni tanomimashoo.

(Let's ask whoever comes early tomorrow morning to do it; that is, the person who has come early and is there.)

Kondo itta toki shashin-o totte-kimasu.

(I will take pictures when I go there next time; that is, when I have finished going and have arrived there.)

If you said *hayaku kuru hito,* it would mean "the person who is expected to come early" instead of "the person who has come early." In the same way, *kondo iku toki* refers to the time when you are on the way to the place, so it should be followed by a phrase such as

. . . *kamera-o motte-ikimasu.*

(I will take a camera with me.)

or

. . . *issho-ni doo-desu-ka.*

(Would you like to go with me?)

noni used to indicate unexpectedness or dissatisfaction

Mr. Lerner and Miss Yoshida took a taxi when they visited Mr. Okada at his office the other day. The traffic was rather heavy and they had to take a detour. Mr. Lerner commented

Michi-ga semai-keredomo, kuruma-ga ooi-desu-ne.
(Although the roads are narrow, there are many cars running.)

Miss Yoshida agreed and said

Honto. Michi-ga konna-ni semai-noni.
(That's right. Even though the roads are so narrow.)

*　　*　　*

Both *keredo(mo)* and *noni* are used to connect two phrases that are opposed to each other in meaning, as in

Haru-ni natta-keredo mada samui.
(Although it's spring now, it's still cold.)
Yakusoku-shita-noni kimasen-deshita.
(He didn't come even though he had promised.)

If you exchange *noni* and *keredomo* in the above sentences, the meaning does not change, but this will indicate a different attitude on the speaker's part. When *noni* is used, the speaker wants to indicate such feelings as surprise, unexpectedness, dissatisfaction or a mixture of these. When Miss Yoshida said

Michi-ga konna-ni semai-noni.
道が　こんなに　せまいのに。

she wanted to indicate her dissatisfaction with the traffic conditions.

Thus *noni* is often used in complaint or blame, as in

Nedan-ga takai-noni oishiku nai.
(Although the price is high, it is not delicious.)
Isshookenmee benkyoo-shita-noni umaku naranai.
(Although I have studied very hard, I haven't improved.)

It is also used to express regret in such set expressions as

Sekkaku oide-kudasaimashita-noni nanno okamai-mo dekimasen-de . . .
(I'm sorry I couldn't do anything to entertain you when you came all this way to see me.)
Taishita oyaku-nimo tachimasen-noni, konna mono-o itadaite-wa mooshiwake arimasen.
(This is too much. I shouldn't accept it — *lit.* I would have no apology to offer if I accepted such a gift when I didn't do much to help you.)

Watashi-ga vs. *Watashi-wa*

Yesterday afternoon Mr. Lerner and Mr. Takada went to Mr. Okada's office together. When they bought their tickets at the subway station, Mr. Takada did not have any small change and Mr. Lerner bought a ticket for him. After they got off the train and started walking on the platform, Mr. Takada asked him *Raanaa-san, kippu-wa?* (Mr. Lerner, what about the ticket?) Mr. Lerner had the two tickets with him, so he answered

Watashi-wa motte-imasu.

meaning "I have them." Then Mr. Takada looked worried, and started looking through his pockets for his ticket.

* * *

To the question "Do you have the tickets?" a Japanese would usually answer *Motte-imasu* because *kippu* has already been mentioned and is understood. *Watashi-wa* is not necessary in this case. Since Mr. Lerner said *Watashi-wa* when it was not necessary, it sounded as if he meant "*I* have *my* ticket," implying "you may not have yours," and therefore Mr. Takada was confused.

It is misleading to use *watashi-wa* when it is not necessary. Similarly, if someone has asked you if you like sumo and you answer *Watashi-wa suki-desu,* it would imply that someone else does not like it. When the question obviously concerns you, it is best not to say *watashi-wa*.

Mr. Lerner could have also said *Watashi-ga motte-imasu,* and Mr. Takada would have understood him correctly. When the question concerns who did or is doing an action in relation to a particular situation, *wa* is used with the situation and *ga* with the agent. For instance, one will often say things like

Kore-wa haha-ga tsukutte-kureta-n-desu.
(As for this, my mother made it for me.)
Kono e-wa dare-ga kaita-n-desu-ka.
(As for this picture, who painted it?)

If one is answering a question, the *wa* phrase is usually left out in the answer, as in

A: *Jisho-wa doko-desu-ka.*
(Where is the dictionary?)
B: *Sakki Yamada-san-ga motte-ikimashita.*
(Mr. Yamada took it somewhere a while ago.)

Thus, in Mr. Lerner's case, he could have answered Mr. Takada's question with

Watashi-ga motte-imasu.
(As for it, I have it with me.)

... *te* used to end a sentence

Mr. Okada came a little late to his appointment yesterday afternoon. He apologized politely by saying

> *Doomo osoku narimashite . . .*
> どうも　おそく　なりまして……
> (I'm sorry I'm late — *lit.* I am late and. . .)

Mr. Lerner remembered then that Mr. Okada very often ended his sentences with . . . *te* and wondered if this was common.

*   *   *

Phrases ending in the *te* form of a verb or adjective are very often used to end a sentence, especially when thanking or apologizing. The basic form used for expressing gratitude is . . . *te arigatoo (-gozaimasu)* (Thank you for . . . ing), as in

> *Oide-kudasatte arigatoo-gozaimasu.*
> (Thank you for coming.)

And the basic expressions of apology are . . . *te sumimasen/mooshiwake arimasen/gomen-nasai/shitsuree-shimashita,* as in

> *Omatase-shite mooshiwake arimasen.*
> (I'm very sorry to have kept you waiting.)

In these expressions, what follows the . . . *te* form is often left out. Especially when one bows, the last part of the sentence is said softly or omitted.

Besides these set expressions, sentences are often ended with . . . *te* or . . . *te-ne* in conversation. When speaking in a familiar tone, one would say

Kinoo-wa sukkari kaeri-ga osoku natte-ne. . .
(I went home quite late yesterday.)
Ano-hito-ga dooshite-mo yaritai-tte iidashite-ne. . .
(He said he wanted very much to do it.)

In polite conversation, . . . *mashite* is used in place of . . . *te* as in

Kinoo-wa sukkari kaeri-ga osoku narimashite. . .

Ending one's sentence with *te* or *te-ne* is often used in a conversation in which both the speaker and the listener participate in making a flow of speech. Namely, when the speaker has said . . . *te (-ne)*, the listener will give *aizuchi* (response words) such as *ee* or *un*. Endings in . . . *te (-ne)* invite and encourage the listener to say something by way of completing the unfinished statement.

... *na* used for the negative imperative

Mr. Takada answered a telephone call from someone and when he finished talking, hurriedly went to where Miss Yoshida was putting some documents into envelopes, and said

Sore-wa mada okuru-na-tte.

Mr. Lerner understood from her reaction that Mr. Takada had told her not to send some of the papers, but he didn't fully understand the usage of *na* in *okuru-na.*

* * *

In social situations the plain imperative form is not commonly used, except in conversation between good friends or family members. Namely, to tell someone to wait, one usually says *Matte-kudasai* rather than using the plain imperative form *Mate!* (Wait!). But in conveying someone's message one uses the plain form even in polite conversation, as in

Mate-to osshaimashita.
(He told me to wait.)
Haha-ga kaette-koi-to iimashita-node. . .
(Since my mother told me to come home. . .)

To convey a negative command, *na* is added to the dictionary form of the verb as in *Matsu-na* (Don't wait), *Kaette-kuru-na* (Don't come back) or *Okuru-na* (Don't send it). These expressions are not used by themselves except in familiar conversation, but they are often used to convey someone's message in polite conversation. When Mr. Takada said *Okuru-na-tte,* he meant "He told us not to send

it''; *tte* is a contraction of *to itta* (he said that . . .).
Another example of this negative form is

>*Tabako-wa suu-na-to oishasan-ni iwaremashita.*
>(I was told by the doctor not to smoke.)

In signs and written instructions, however, the plain forms are often preferred, as in

>*Wataru-na.*
>わたるな。
>(Don't cross. — road sign)
>*Kiken. Fureru-na.*
>(Danger. Don't touch. — sign on a machine)

In this case, the plain negative imperative sounds more direct than using polite expressions like *Wataranaide-kudasai* (Please don't cross) or *Watatte-wa ikemasen* (You should not cross).

... *na* used for a familiar command

Mr. Lerner was invited to the Takadas' home last Saturday. When they were having dinner, their five-year-old son started playing around with his food instead of eating it. Mr. Takada noticed this and said

Ken-chan, hayaku tabena.
(Ken, eat your food — *lit.* eat quickly.)

Mr. Lerner understood that this was an order or mild reprimand, but he had not learned the expression *tabena,* and felt that it was rather confusing as it sounded like the *na* used for the negative imperative.

*　　*　　*

Tabena is a command, meaning "Eat it." This *na,* like *nasai* in *Tabenasai* (Eat it), is added to the stem (the form preceding ... *masu; tabemasu* — *tabe*), while the *na* for the negative imperative is added to the dictionary form (*taberu*). Therefore the two are not confused.

This "stem plus *na*" is used as a familiar command, and is not used in social situations. The form ... *nasai* cannot be used to someone you should talk politely to, except in set expressions like *Okaeri-nasai* (Welcome home) or *Oyasumi-nasai* (Good night). This ... *na* form is even more familiar than ... *nasai* and is used only between family members or good friends. Parents will often use it to their young children. Sometimes *yo* is added to soften the tone when used toward children, as in

Ii ko-da-kara, moo yoshina-yo.
(Be a good boy and stop it.)

Women often prefer ... *te-ne* when giving commands to children, as in *Tabete-ne* (Eat it, will you?) or *Moo yoshite-ne.*

And this ... *na* form is often used to persuade others in a very familiar tone in vulgar speech. It actually reminds many Japanese of Tora-san, a famous movie character, telling this sister:

Ore-no koto-wa ii-kara, danna-o daiji-ni shite-yarina-yo.

(Don't bother about me. Just take good care of your man.)

... *te-wa* used for indicating condition

Mr. Lerner and Miss Yoshida planned a party and most of the colleagues they invited said that they would come, but Mr. Kobayashi, a very good socializer, said that he couldn't. When they talked about this later, Miss Yoshida looked disappointed and said

Kobayashi-san-ga konakute-wa omoshiroku naranai-wane.
(If Mr. Kobayashi doesn't come, the party won't be fun.)

Mr. Lerner agreed and said

Ee, Kobayashi-san-ga konakute-wa yamemashoo-ka.

meaning "If he doesn't come, shall we call it off?" Miss Yoshida didn't correct him, but he felt the expression *konakute-wa* sounded wrong somehow.

* * *

The pattern "verb plus ... *te-wa/de-wa*" is used, like ... *eba,* to indicate a condition, as in

Kuraku natte-wa dekimasen.
(We can't do it if it becomes dark.)
Kuraku nareba dekimasen.
(We can't do it if it becomes dark.)

However ... *te-wa* is limited to cases when what follows is in the negative form or has a negative meaning. Namely, after *Kuraku natte-wa* you can say such things as:

... *dekimasen*. (. . . we can't do it.)
... *kiken-desu*. (. . . it's dangerous.)
... *dame-desu*. (. . . it won't do.)

but you cannot say

... *tsugoo-ga ii*. (. . . it's convenient for us.)

Another limitation is that this can be used only when what follows indicates the speaker's judgment; it cannot be used before the description of an action like *yamemasu* or *yamemasen*.

Since . . . *te-wa* is associated with the speaker's negative judgment, there are several set expressions like . . . *te-wa ikemasen* (you shouldn't . . .), . . . *te-wa dame-desu* (you shouldn't. . .), and . . . *te-wa komarimasu* (I wish you wouldn't . . .) which are used to express an admonition or complaint, as in

Sonna koto-o shite-wa ikemasen.
そんな　ことを　しては　いけません。
(You shouldn't do such a thing — *lit*. If you do such a thing, it won't do.)
Soko-e okarete-wa komarimasu.
(I wish you wouldn't put it there — *lit*. If you put it there, I will be distressed — *okarete* is an example of the so-called suffering passive, meaning "I will suffer if you put it . . .").

Chan-to used to express expectations

The other day a meeting was held at Mr. Lerner's office with several people coming in from outside. When everybody was there, Mr. Lerner went to tell Mr. Mori, the director of the company, that they were ready. Mr. Mori then asked him about one of the more important persons who usually came late. Mr. Lerner answered

Hai, chan-to irasshaimashita.

meaning "Yes, he came exactly on time." But Mr. Mori laughed, to his surprise.

*　　　*　　　*

The word *chan-to* is usually defined as "exactly" or "precisely" in the dictionary, but this word cannot be used in social situations to refer to someone who should be respected.

Chan-to expresses the idea that someone does or did his duty just in the way expected of him by the speaker. It is very commonly used by mothers with their children as in

Chan-to fuku-o kinasai.
(Dress yourself properly.)
Gohan-wa chan-to tabenasai.
(Eat your meal(s) properly.)

The second example above differs in meaning depending on the situation. When a mother says it to her child who is playing around with his food, it means "Eat properly," but when she says it to her son who says he is too busy to have lunch, it means "Have your meals regularly." Since *chan-to* expresses the speaker's expectations, one has to know what the speaker expects to understand the exact meaning of this word.

Because *chan-to* implies the speaker's evaluation or judgment of someone's actions, it is impolite to say things like

> *Chan-to jikan-ni kite-kudasai.*
> (Please come exactly on time.)
> *Chan-to irasshaimashita.*

unless the listener or person referred to is younger or in a lower position. When Mr. Lerner said *Chan-to irasshaimashita* to refer to a VIP, Mr. Mori thought it humorous. In this kind of situation, one should just say

> *Hai, irasshaimashita.*
> (Yes, he's here.)

avoiding any expression that may imply the speaker's expectations or judgment. If the time of arrival is important, one can say something like

> *Hai, gofun-hodo mae-ni irasshaimashita.*
> (Yes, he came about five minutes ago.)

Expressions of pleasure

Yesterday afternoon Mr. Mori, the director of the company, thanked Mr. Lerner for a proposal of his for management improvement, saying that it had worked out very well. Mr. Lerner was very pleased to hear that, so he said

Taihen yorokobimasu.

meaning "I'm very happy about it." But after saying that, Mr. Lerner wondered if he should have said

Ureshii-desu.

instead.

*   *   *

The word *yorokobu* means "to rejoice," "to be happy about something"; it is used in sentences like

Shiken-ga nakunatta-node gakusee-tachi-wa yorokonde-iru.
(Since the test has been suspended, the students are very happy.)
Sore-o kiitara kanai-mo yorokobu-deshoo.
(My wife will be happy to hear that.)

It is usually used to refer to someone else's pleasure so that if you just say

Yorokobimasu.

it will sound as if someone else is happy.

To express one's pleasure directly, *ureshii* is used, as in

TV interviewer: *Gokansoo-wa?* (How do you feel?)
Match winner: *Ureshii-desu, totemo.* (I'm so happy.)

Ureshii can be used in an emotional situation like this, or in conversation between good friends or family members, as a direct expression of one's feelings. However, the Japanese regard it as good to refrain from directly expressing one's feelings in social situations. In a situation like Mr. Lerner's above, one would normally say something like

Oyaku-ni tatte yokatta-to omoimasu.
(I am glad I could be of some help to you.)

Or he could thank him and attribute the merit to someone else, as in

Arigatoo-gozaimasu. Minasan-no okage-desu.
(Thank you. I managed it thanks to everybody's kindness.)

Suru used to mean 'to cost'

Yesterday morning Mr. Takada admired Mr. Lerner's tie and said

Sore, zuibun shita-deshoo.
それ、ずいぶん　したでしょう。

Mr. Lerner didn't understand that at first. He wondered if Mr. Takada had meant "You must have worn it for a long time," because *suru* can mean "to wear a tie." Then Miss Yoshida joined them and said

Takakatta-deshoo-ne.
(It must have been very expensive.)

so Mr. Lerner remembered that *suru* can also mean "to cost."

*　　　*　　　*

The verb *suru* (to do) has various meanings since it is a basic verb like the English "do." When it is preceded by an amount of money, it means "to cost," as in

Ikura shimashita-ka.
(How much did it cost?)
Ichiman-en-mo shita-n-desu.
(It cost me as much as ¥10,000.)
Nisen-en-shika shimasen-deshita.
(It cost me only ¥2,000.)

It is also used in this sense with words indicating degree, as in

Zuibun shimashita.
(It cost me a great deal.)

Amari shimasen-deshita.
(It didn't cost me much.)

In the last two examples, however, *suru* can mean "to do something" instead of "to cost" depending on the situation, as in

A: *Zuibun renshuu-shita-n-deshoo.*
(You must have practiced a great deal.)
B: *Iie, jikan-ga nakute, amari shimasen-deshita.*
(No, I didn't have much time so I didn't practice very much.)

The pronunciation, as well as the situation, helps prevent ambiguity; to mean "to cost much," *zuibun* and *shita* are pronounced together as one phrase without any pause between them.

This distinction also applies to another use of *suru*, namely to mean "to behave" when used with such adverbs as *yukkuri* (leisurely), *nonbiri* (in a relaxed manner) and *burabura* (strolling, loafing), which describe actions. If your host says

Yukkuri-shite-itte-kudasai.

it means "Please make yourself at home and stay as long as you like." Saying

Yasumi-da-kara nonbiri-shite-imasu.

means "I am taking it easy because today is a holiday." But if someone says

Sono shigoto-wa isogimasen-kara, yukkuri shite-kudasai.

it means "Since there is no hurry for that work, please take your time in doing it."

Moshika-suru-to used to indicate uncertainty

When Mr. Lerner and his colleagues were discussing their plans for going plum-blossom viewing, Mr. Takada wondered if it might not rain that day. Miss Yoshida said

Ee, moshika-suru-to-ne.
(Yes, maybe.)

Then they discussed what to do if it did turn out to be a rainy day. Mr. Lerner wondered what degree of probability is implied by *moshika-suru-to.*

* * *

Moshika-suru-to or *moshika-shitara* indicates that the speaker is not certain about something happening although he thinks there is some possibility of it. Sentences including this word normally end with *kamo shirenai* (may), as in

Moshika-suru-to kono takara-kuji ataru-kamo shiremasen-yo.
(This lottery ticket may win a prize.)
Mada unten-ga heta-da-kara, moshika-shitara kootsuu-jiko-o okosu-kamo shirenai.
(Since he is not good at driving yet, he may cause a traffic accident.)

There are several other expressions used in a similar way such as *koto-ni yoru-to* which sounds more formal, *hyotto-suru-to* which is less common, and *arui-wa* which sounds much more formal than *moshika-suru-to.*

Tabun is another word often used to indicate probability. When compared with *moshika-suru-to, tabun* implies that the speaker is pretty certain, and the sentence usually ends with *deshoo* or *daroo,* as in

Ano-hito-no koto-da-kara, tabun okurete kuru-deshoo.
(Since he is such a person, he will probably come late — *literally,* Since it is a matter of that person, he will probably come late.)

Since *moshika-suru-to* implies that the speaker is uncertain, it has the function of expressing his consideration or reserve toward the listener. For instance, when the speaker is reluctant to disappoint the listener, he will say

Moshika-suru-to korarenai-kamo shiremasen.
もしかすると　来られないかも　しれません。
(I'm afraid I may not be able to come.)

Or he may use it when referring to something unpleasant, as in

A: *Kondo-wa umaku ikanai yoona ki-ga suru-n-desu.*
(I feel somehow it won't go well.)
B: *Soo-desu-nee. Moshika-suru-to soo-kamo shiremasen-ne.*
(Well, I'm afraid it may not.)

desu-mono used to mean 'since' or 'for'

Miss Yoshida seemed so busy yesterday evening that Mr. Lerner wondered if she couldn't ask Mrs. Hayashi to help her, but she said

Hayashi-san-niwa chotto-ne .... Shinkon-desu-mono.
(I can't very well ask Mrs. Hayashi since she's a newlywed.)

Mr. Lerner wondered if *Shinkon-desu-mono* is the same as *Shinkon-desu-kara,* and if the former sounds more feminine.

* * *

Women often use *... desu-mono* or *... mono* to indicate a reason, as in

Ashita-wa ginkoo-wa oyasumi-yo. Doyoobi-desu-mono.
(The banks will be closed tomorrow since it is Saturday.)
Kawanai-wa. Datte okane-ga nai-mono.
(I won't buy it since I don't have the money.)

In this usage *mono* comes after some statement which it supports. Men also use it with *da,* as in *doyoobi-da-mono,* but only in conversation with good friends or family members.

This usage is rather limited because it has an implication that the speaker is trying to defend himself; it is not appropriate in social situations. It is limited to conversations where self-defense is allowed, or to cases when self-justification can be polite, as in

A: *Gomeewaku-o okake-shite, mooshiwake arimasen.*

(I'm very sorry to trouble you.)

B: *Iie, sonna koto-wa arimasen. Watashi-no shigoto-desu-mono.*

(No, you have no reason to feel sorry since that is part of my job.)

In such cases as this too, *desu-mono* can be used only by women; men will say *shigoto-desu-kara* instead.

Some people say that such expressions as *desu-mono* are feminine expressions, but it would be more accurate to say that they belong to what could be called family language, as opposed to social language. Up to now women have been regarded as mostly living at home, but as society changes, the usage of this type of expression will also change.

koto used to mean 'necessity'

When Mr. Lerner and his colleagues were leaving the office yesterday evening, Mr. Kato was still working. Miss Yoshida wondered if he wasn't working too hard, and Mr. Takada approached him and said

> *Sonna-ni osoku-made yaru koto-wa nai-daroo.*
> そんなに おそくまで やる ことは ないだろう。

Mr. Lerner understood that he was advising Mr. Kato to stop working, but he did not know exactly what the word *koto* stood for; he wondered if it meant "work" and that there wasn't so much work that he had to stay that late.

*   *   *

The word *koto* is used in various ways and sometimes it is very difficult for foreigners to understand what it means. Basically *koto* stands for "a fact" or "a thing" as in

> *Kyoo-wa nanimo suru koto-ga nakute taikutsu-desu.*
> (I don't have anything to do today, so I am bored.)
> *Ano-hito-ga yameta koto, shitte-imasu-ka.*
> (Do you know the fact that he quit?)

Besides this, *koto* is used in idiomatic expressions such as . . . *suru koto-ga aru* (sometimes do . . .), . . . *shita koto-ga aru* (to have the experience of doing . . .), . . . *koto-ni naru* (it is decided to do . . .), *koto-ni suru* (to decide on doing . . .). For example:

> *Jibun-de shokuji-o tsukuru koto-mo arimasu.*

(I sometimes cook my own meals.)
Ichido-dake ano-hito-ni atta koto-ga arimasu.
(I have met him just once.)
Ashita kaigi-o suru koto-ni narimashita.
(It has been decided to hold a meeting tomorrow.)
Hikkosu koto-ni shimashita.
(We decided to move to another house.)

In Mr. Takada's statement, *koto* was used in the sense of "necessity"; what he meant was "There isn't any necessity for you to work so late, is there?" This usage is rather common, and is generally followed by the negative (*nai, arimasen,* etc.) as in

Anna hito-no tame-ni kuroo-suru koto-wa arimasen-yo.
(You don't have to go to special trouble for the sake of a person like him.)
Boku-ga wazawaza iku koto-wa nai-daroo. Ittatte yaku-ni tatanai-mono.
(There's no need for me to go all the way there. I wouldn't be of much help anyway.)

tokoro used to mean 'situation'

When Mr. Lerner came back to the office from a business trip at around three yesterday afternoon, Miss Yoshida said

Choodo ii tokoro-e kaette-kimashita-ne.
ちょうど いい ところへ 帰ってきましたね。
(You came back just at the right moment.)

and started preparing tea for him, for everyone was having tea and a sweet at that time. Mr. Lerner wondered if *tokoro* is often used to mean "time" rather than "place."

*   *   *

The word *tokoro* means "place" as in

Shinjuku-wa nigiyakana tokoro-desu.
(Shinjuku is lively — *lit*. Shinjuku is a lively place.)
Sakki oita tokoro-ni miatarimasen.
(I can't find it in the place where I left it.)

Besides this usage, it is often used to refer to a time or situation rather than a concrete place, as in

Kore-kara dekakeru tokoro-desu.
(I am about to leave.)
Ima kaette-kita tokoro-desu.
(I have just now come back.)

In the above two sentences, the speaker is referring to a situation where an action is going to take place or has been completed. When Miss Yoshida said *ii tokoro,* she was referring to the situation where everybody was going to have tea and a sweet. In

100

the same way, one can use *warui tokoro* as in

Warui tokoro-o kachoo-ni mirarete-shimatta. Inemuri-shite-ta-n-da-yo.

which means that the section chief saw the speaker in an embarrassing situation because he was nodding over his work.

When used with ... *te-iru*, it implies that someone is in the midst of an action, as in

Ima kigae-o shite-iru tokoro-desu-kara, soto-de matte-ite-kudasai.

(I'm changing my clothes now, so please wait outside.)

There are several other expressions including *tokoro* such as ... *ta tokoro-de* (even if) and *moo sukoshi-de ... (suru) tokoro-datta* (almost ...), as in

Ima-kara itta tokoro-de ma-ni aimasen-yo.

(You won't be in time if you go now.)

Moo sukoshi-de korobu tokoro-datta.

(I almost stumbled — *lit*. If I had been a little more unlucky, I would have stumbled.)

Referring to someone else's wishes

Mr. Lerner discussed various things with Mr. Mori, the director of the company, at his office yesterday afternoon. When he was leaving, Mr. Mori asked him to tell Miss Yoshida to come to see him. He went to her and told her

Shachoo-ga aitagatte-irasshaimasu.

meaning "The director would like to see you." She thanked him and immediately went to Mr. Mori, but Mr. Lerner somehow felt that the Japanese was not fully appropriate.

*   *   *

There are several rules about referring to someone else's wishes. One rule is that the . . . *tai* form is not used; this form is used mostly about the speaker himself as in *Aitai-to omoimasu* (I would like to see her). It is wrong to say *Ano-hito-wa aitai-desu* (He wants to see her). Instead, one should use . . . *tagaru* with the third person as in

Imooto-mo aitagatte-imasu.
(My sister wants to see her, too.)

Mr. Lerner was right in that he used . . . *tagaru* rather than . . . *tai* when referring to someone else's wishes.

But you have to follow another rule that . . . *tagaru* cannot be used to refer to someone about whom you have to be polite. The expression . . . *tagaru* is used to vividly describe how anxiously someone is to do something. If you say *ikitagatte-imasu,* for instance, it sounds as if the person is so anxious to go that he can hardly sit still. To be polite, one should refrain from describing someone behaving in such an emotional way. Thus, . . . *tagaru* can be used only to refer to younger people or someone you don't have to be polite about. For this reason *aitagatte-iru* was not appropriate here because it sounds as if the director were begging his girlfriend to meet him.

To refer to someone's wishes politely, it is better to refer to his action rather than his wishes. This means that you should avoid using either . . . *tai* or . . . *tagaru* and choose some completely different expression. Instead of *aitagatte-iru,* Mr. Lerner should have said something like

Shachoo-ga oyobi-desu.
社長が　お呼びです。
(*lit.* The director is calling for you.)

... *te-itadaku* to express gratitude

The editor of an English-language magazine asked Mr. Lerner to write about his experiences in Japan, which he did last month. Recently the magazine came out, so he handed several copies out to his colleagues asking them to read his article and give him their opinions about it. When he met Mr. Mori this morning, he asked him

Ano kiji, oyomi-ni narimashita-ka.
(Did you read the article?)

Mr. Mori answered yes and gave his impressions of it, but Miss Yoshida later told him that he should have said

Ano kiji, yonde-itadakemashita-ka.
(*lit.* Did you do me the favor of reading it?)

*   *   *

To speak politely, it is necessary to use polite expressions, and also to express one's gratitude or apology when that is due. It is not very polite to say

Yomimashita-ka.
(Did you read it?)

It is more polite to say

Oyomi-ni narimashita-ka.

or

Goran-ni narimashita-ka.

but this is merely verbal politeness. When you are referring to some action that is not related to your personal interests, verbal politeness is sufficient.

For instance, when you want to ask if the other person has read today's newspaper or some news in it, you can appropriately say

Kyoo-no shinbun oyomi-ni narimashita-ka.
Ano nyuusu, goran-ni narimashita-ka.

But when reading something implies doing a favor for you, you should choose other expressions such as

Yonde-kudasaimashita-ka.
or
Yonde-itadakemashita-ka.

which mean "Did you kindly read it for me?" Of these two expressions, ... *te-kudasaimashita-ka* and ... *te-itadakemashita-ka,* the latter is more polite because it implies that you regard the favor as a big one and feel you would be lucky to see it realized. And using *oyomi* instead of *yonde* and adding ... *deshoo-ka* make the expression even more polite. If you want to ask politely whether the other person has read your letter or not, you should say

Tegami-o sashiagemashita-ga, oyomi-itadakemashita-deshoo-ka.
手紙を　さしあげましたが、お読みいただけました でしょうか。
(May I ask if you have read the letter I sent you?)

105

Some contracted forms in rapid speech

Mr. Lerner had some difficulty handling a new computer the other day, and when Mr. Takada came by, he asked for his help, but he said

Wakarya shinai-yo, boku-nanka.

He understood that Mr. Takada did not know much about the computer, but he wondered what *wakarya* means exactly. Is it a contracted form of *wakareba* (if I understand)?

* * *

In rapid speech contracted forms are often used, making it difficult for foreigners to understand. Actually *wakarya* is used as the contraction of two different forms.

1. The ... *i-wa* pattern, as in *wakari-wa shinai,* becomes ... *ya; wakari-wa* becomes *wakarya* and *iki-wa* becomes *ikya.*

2. The ... *eba* (conditional) form becomes *ya; wakareba* becomes *wakarya* and *ikeba* becomes *ikya.* This is limited to the *u* verbs, the *yodan* or *godan* verbs, whose plain negative ends in ... *anai* (eg. *wakaranai, ikanai*). Verbs of the other group, namely those called the *ru* verbs or the *ichidan* verbs have ... *reba* as the conditional form; *okireba* becomes *okirya* and *mireba* becomes *mirya.*

Thus, such verbs as *wakaru* or *iku* have the same contraction for both ... *eba* and ... *i-wa.*

The pattern "stem plus -*wa shinai* or *shimasen*" is used as an emphatic negative. *Wakari-wa shinai* or *wakarya shinai* means "I/he/she/they will never understand." This is what Mr. Takada said.

But another possible interpretation is that he

106

used this in the sense of "if", *wakareba, shinai* could mean "If I did understand, I wouldn't do it." This interpretation is possible if there is a pause between the two phrases.

Thus,

Okane-ga arya-shimasen.
お金が　ありゃしません。

means "I don't have any money at all," while

Okane-ga arya, shimasen.
お金がありゃ、しません。

means "If I did have the money, I wouldn't do it."
When you look at these sentences written down, you may think that they are easy to confuse, but in actual speech, the pronunciation makes the difference clear.

107

Sochira, kochira used as personal pronouns

When Mr. Lerner came back to the office from lunch, Miss Yoshida was talking on the phone. She seemed to be arranging an appointment; she said

Sochira-ga yokereba, kochira-wa kekkoo-desu.
(*lit.* If that direction is okay, this direction is okay.)

Mr. Lerner understood that she meant that if something was all right with the listener she would not mind it, but he wondered if *sochira* and *kochira* can always be used in place of "you" and "I."

*　　　*　　　*

Such words as *kore, kono* and *kochira* are used to refer to something close to the speaker. From this usage, *kochira* is often used to mean "this person" as in

Yoshida-san, kochira-wa Suzuki-san-desu.
(Mr. Yoshida, this is Mrs. Suzuki — said when introducing someone.)

In the same way, *kochira* is used to mean "I" or "we" as in

Kochira-wa nanji-demo kamaimasen.
こちらは　何時でも　かまいません。
(Any time is all right with me/us.)

On the other hand such words as *sore, sono* and *sochira* are used to refer to something close to the listener. From this usage, *sochira* can refer to the listener as in

Kochira-wa kamaimasen-ga, sochira-wa doo-desu-ka.

(We don't mind, but what about you?)

Or, in another example, a telephone conversation,

Son: *Okaasan, genki?*
Mother: *Ee, kochira-wa genki-yo. Sochira-wa?*
Son: *Un, kochira-mo genki-da-yo.*
(Son: How are you, Mom? Mother: I'm fine. How about you? Son: I'm fine, too.)

But this does not mean that *kochira* and *sochira* are used to mean just "I" and "you." *Kochira* actually means "person(s) belonging to this side or my side" and *sochira* means "person(s) belonging to your side." When one uses these words, one is conscious of the contrast between the listener and himself, whether one is actually referring to a single person or to more than one person. They cannot be used as in

Kochira-wa isogashii-desu. (I am busy).
Sochira-wa owarimashita-ka.
(Are you through?)

unless the two sides — the speaker's and the listener's — are being contrasted.

... *ppoi* used to mean '. . . ish'

When Mr. Lerner came back to the office from lunch, Miss Yoshida was complaining about something to Mr. Takada. It seemed that Mr. Mori, the director of the company, did not like the way she had arranged a pack of documents for him and had talked sharply to her. She said

Honto-ni okorippoi-n-desu-mono.
(He loses his temper so easily — *lit.* Really easy to get angry.)

But when Mr. Takada said something to comfort her, she soon started laughing. Mr. Lerner admired the way Mr. Takada put her in a good humor, and at the same time, wondered if he could say *waraippoi* (laughs easily) to describe her.

*　　　*　　　*

The suffix ... *ppoi* can be added to various words. First, it is added to the names of colors as in

shiro (white) — *shiroppoi* (whitish) 白っぽい
kuro (black) — *kuroppoi* (dark) 黒っぽい

You might ask someone what color clothes Mr. So-and-So was wearing, and he will answer

Yoku oboete-imasen-kedo, nandaka kuroppoi fuku-deshita.
(I don't remember well, but I think he wore something dark.)

When ... *ppoi* is added to some nouns, it adds the implication of "too much of . . ." as in *kodomo* (child) — *kodomoppoi* (childish), e.g. *kodomoppoi hito* (a childish person)

mizu (water) — *mizuppoi* (containing too much water), e.g. *mizuppoi misoshiru* (*miso* soup which tastes as if it had been diluted with water)

In this usage, the implication is rather negative. While *kodomo-rashii* (like a child) implies young energy or innocence, *kodomoppoi* implies immaturity.

Sometimes . . . *ppoi* is added to certain verbs which describe emotions such as *okoru* (get angry), *wasureru* (forget) or *higamu* (feel oneself as being treated unfairly). You can say something like

Kono-goro wasureppoku natte komatte-imasu.

(I'm getting so forgetful lately I don't know what to do.)

Toshiyori-wa higamippoi mono-da.

(Old people tend to feel that they are treated unfairly.)

But you cannot add . . . *ppoi* to verbs like *taberu* (eat) or *aruku* (walk), which describe action. Therefore Mr. Lerner was right when he refrained from saying *waraippoi* because *warau* describes an action rather than an emotion.

. . . *dasu* used to mean 'start . . . ing'

When Mr. Lerner was getting ready to leave the office yesterday evening, he noticed that it had started raining, so he said

Ame-ga furihajimemashita.

meaning "It has started raining." Then Miss Yoshida also looked out the window and said

Honto. Zuibun hayaku furidashimashita-ne.
(That's right. It has started raining much earlier than expected.)

Mr. Lerner wondered what difference there is between *furihajimeru* and *furidasu*. He felt that the Japanese often used . . . *dasu* where he would use . . . *hajimeru.*

*　　　*　　　*

The verb *dasu* (to take out) is added to other verbs to add the meaning of "to start" or "out."

With verbs referring to the action of moving or taking something to other places, . . . *dasu* adds the meaning of "out." For instance, *mochidasu* means "to bring out," and *nagedasu* means "to throw out," *hakobidasu* "to carry out." With other verbs, . . . *dasu* adds the meaning of "to start" as in *furidasu*, which Miss Yoshida used in the remark above.

Both *hajimeru* and *dasu* mean "to start," and very often both of them can be added to the same verb; one says either *furihajimeru* or *furidasu*, and either *kuraku narihajimeru* (to start to become dark) or *kuraku naridasu*. There is very little difference in meaning between . . . *hajimeru* and . . .

dasu, except that verbs with ... *dasu* sound more conversational. If you compare the two sentences

  Nihongo-o hanasu gaikokujin-ga fuehajimeta.
  (The number of foreigners who speak Japanese has begun to increase.)

and
  Nihongo-o hanasu gaikokujin-ga fuedashita.

the second sounds more conversational, although they mean the same thing.

  However, ... *dasu* is preferred with verbs which indicate sudden change or unexpected occurrence. For instance, *okoridasu* (to get angry), *nakidasu* (to break out crying), and *waraidasu* (to break out laughing) are usually used instead of *okorihajimeru; nakihajimeru* and *waraihajimeru,* as in

  Ano-hito, kyuu-ni okoridashite, kaetchatta.
  あの人、きゅうに　おこりだして、帰っちゃった。
  (She suddenly got angry and left.)

  Another difference between ... *dasu* and ... *hajimeru* is that ... *hajimeru* is preferred when making requests or proposals, as in

  Kuji-ni nattara kakihajimete-kudasai.
  (Please start writing at nine.)
  Sorosoro katazukehajimemashoo-ka.
  (Shall we start cleaning up?)

Expressions meaning 'Not all . . .'

Mr. Lerner told Miss Yoshida about an outing he had enjoyed with several of his colleagues the past weekend. Miss Yoshida asked him if all that first planned to go actually went, so he answered.

Minna ikimasen-deshita.

meaning "Not all of them went." But Miss Yoshida looked puzzled for a moment. He realized that he had again failed in appropriately expressing the meaning of the English "not all. . . ."

*   *   *

Using such words as *minna* (all) and *zenbu* (all) with a negative expression sounds ambiguous. *Minna ikimasen-deshita* is not commonly used; it can mean "Nobody went." Most Japanese would choose other expressions for this purpose such as

Daremo ikimasen-deshita. (Nobody went.)
Hitori-mo kimasen-deshita.
(Not any of them came.)

to clearly mean "None of them . . ." In the same way, if you say

Zenbu, yomimasen-deshita.

it would sound as if you didn't read any of it.

To mean "not all . . .," Japanese use several expressions. One is to add *wa* after the word meaning "all" as in

Zenbu-wa yomimasen-deshita.
(I didn't read all of it.)

114

Zen'in-wa ikimasen-deshita.
(Not all of the members went.)

(But *minna-wa* is usually avoided, because *minna-wa . . .* often implies "everybody did . . .")

Besides adding *wa*, Japanese use *. . . n-ja arimasen* or *wake-ja arimasen* to mean "not all. . ." Mr. Lerner could have said

Minna itta-n-ja arimasen.
Minna itta wake-ja arimasen.
みんな　行った　わけじゃ　ありません。

And there are several other expressions used depending on the situation. For instance, when the speaker wants to emphasize that the amount did not reach the maximum, he would use *tokoro* as in

Zenbu yomu-to yuu tokoro-made-wa ikimasen-deshita.
(I could not go so far as to read all of it.)

Or, when the speaker wants to say that the amount is too great to finish, he will use *. . . kirenai* (cannot finish) as in

Tabekiremasen-deshita.
(I couldn't eat all of it.)
Jikan-ga nakute, yomikiremasen-deshita.
(Because the time was short, I couldn't read all of it.)

Expressions used for strong denial

Mr. Takada always brings a lunch that his wife fixes for him. Someone looked at his lunch and admired it yesterday, and teasingly asked Miss Yoshida if she could make such a good lunch. She answered calmly

Sonna koto, dekikko nai-desho.
そんな　こと、できっこ　ないでしょ。

Mr. Lerner wondered if *dekikko nai* means the same thing as *dekiru hazu-ga nai* (one can never do it).

* * *

The . . . *kko* is said to have come from *koto* (a fact), but in the present usage it indicates a strong denial when added to the stem of a verb as in *dekikko nai* or *wakarikko nai* (one can never understand it). By saying *Sonna koto, dekikko nai-desho,* Miss Yoshida meant "How could I possibly do such a thing?"

This expression is similar to . . . *hazu-ga nai* in that it indicates a negative judgment. Both indicate the speaker's strong denial, but the difference is that . . . *kko nai* sounds more familiar and cannot be used in formal situations.

Another expression of strong denial used in familiar speech is . . . *mon(o)-ka* or . . . *mon(o)-desu-ka.* Miss Yoshida could have used it and said

Sonna koto dekiru mon-desu-ka.

This is a rhetorical question and is said with a falling tone. A man will say

Sonna koto dekiru mon-ka.

in familiar conversation. Since this is a direct expression of one's feeling, it cannot be used in polite situations when one has to show reserve.

In polite speech, one usually avoids any flat, strong denial and says just ... *nai-to omoimasu.* Miss Yoshida would say, in the presence of someone like the director of the company, something like

Sore-wa dekinai-to omoimasu.

Sonna implies a negative evaluation and so it is usually avoided in reserved speech.

Hanasu (speak) and *hanashikakeru* (speak to)

When Mr. Lerner and his colleagues were having tea during their lunch hour, someone asked him if there was anything he disliked about living in Japan. He does not like to be spoken to in English by a Japanese he does not know when he wants to be alone, so he said.

Shiranai hito-ga eego-de hanasu-noga iya-desu-ne.

Everybody understood but Miss Yoshida later told him that he should have said

Shiranai hito-ni eego-de hanashikakerareru-noga iya-desu-ne.

instead. *Hanashikakerareru* seemed to be a terribly long word, and he wondered if any shorter word could be used instead.

*　　　*　　　*

The word *hanasu* means "to speak," but it means "to talk with someone" rather than "to speak to someone." To mean "to speak to someone" usually *kakeru* is added as in

Unten-chuu-ni hanashikakeru-to abunai-desu.
(It is dangerous to speak to someone when he is driving.)

To mean "I was spoken to," . . . *rareru* is added as in

Densha-no naka-de shiranai hito-ni hanashikakeraremashita.
(A stranger spoke to me on the train — *lit.* I

118

was spoken to by a stranger.)

... *ga* ... *te-kuru* is also used in place of the passive ending ... *rareru*. Namely, you can also say

Shiranai hito-ga hanashikakete-kimashita.
(A stranger spoke to me.)

... *kakeru* is often added to the stem of verbs and gives the meaning of "to start doing something," as in

Yomikakemashita-ga owarimasen-deshita.
(I started to read it but didn't finish it.)
Yarikaketa shigoto-ga arimasu-node, chotto matte-ite-kudasaimasen-ka.
(Would you please wait a moment as I have just started doing something?)

In this way, *hanashikakeru* can also mean "to start speaking," but usually there is no possibility of misunderstanding because the meaning is clear from the context.

119

Expressions ending in ... *nasai*

Mr. Lerner wanted Mr. Mori, the director of the company, to look at an article in a magazine. He used the expression *goran-ni naru,* the honorific version of *miru,* and said

Doozo goran-nasai.

meaning "Please look at it," but he felt that this was somehow inappropriate and changed it to

Goran-ni natte-kudasai.
*   *   *

... *nasai* usually indicates a command to a younger person. A mother or teacher will often use it with children as in

Hayaku okinasai. (Get up quickly.)
Ki-o tsukenasai. (Be careful.)

One cannot use ... *nasai* in polite requests except in set expressions such as *Okaerinasai* (Welcome home) and *Oyasuminasai* (Good night). Even with such expressions, sometimes one adds *mase* to make them sound more polite, as in *Okaerinasai-mase* and *Oyasuminasai-mase.*

The expression *goran-ni naru* is polite, used as in

Ano eega, moo goran-ni narimashita-ka.
(Have you seen that movie?)

To use it in a request you can say either

Goran-ni natte-kudasai (masen-ka).

or, more concisely, *Goran-kudasai*. But it is not polite to use . . . *nasai* as in *Goran-nasai*.

When making a polite request, it is good to add *kudasaimasen-ka* either as in

> *Goran-ni natte-kudasaimasen-ka.*

or

> *Goran-kudasaimasen-ka.*

In the same way, the most appropriate expressions for politely asking someone to come are either

> *Oide-ni natte-kudasaimasen-ka.*

or

> *Oide-kudasaimasen-ka.*

... *komu* used to mean 'into'

The trains were particularly crowded yesterday morning; when he arrived at the office, Mr. lerner felt quite tired. He explained how crowded the trains were, saying

Eki-de ushiro-kara osaremashita.
(I was pushed from behind at the station.)

Miss Yoshida remarked that it must have been dangerous, but he answered that it was good because he could get into the train. She said

Aa, oshikomareta-n-desu-ne.
(Oh, you were pushed into the train.)

Mr. Lerner realized that *osareru* and *oshikomareru* are quite different, and wondered if he could use *komu* with other verbs in the same way.

*　　　*　　　*

While *osu* means "to push someone/something," *oshikomu* means "to push someone/something into a certain place." ... *komu* adds the meaning of "into" when attached to the stem of certain verbs. For instance, one may say to a person who is cramming his bag with too many things,

Sonna-ni takusan oshikomu-to kaban-ga itamimasu-yo.
(You will damage your bag if you put too many things into it.)

In the same way, while *kakeru* means "to run," *kakekomu* means "to run into some place" as in

Osoku natta-node, kaisha-made kakete itta.
(Since I was late, I ran to the office.)
Osoroshikatta-node, kooban-ni kakekomi-mashia.
(Since I was frightened, I ran into a police box.)

Sometimes *komu* adds the meaning of "deeply" or "intent." For instance, saying *Kaisha-no mae-de suwatte imasu* means "They are sitting in front of the office," but

Kaisha-no mae-de suwarikonde-imasu.

means "They are sitting in front of the office in protest." And

Sukkari hanashite-shimaimashita.

means "I told you everything," but when a visitor says to a host

Sukkari hanashikonde-shimaimashita.

it means "I stayed too long because I was absorbed in the conversation."

123

Use of ... *desu*, ... *deshita*

When they met Monday morning, Mr. Okada asked Mr. Lerner

Kinoo-wa dokoka-e odekake-deshita-ka.
きのうは　どこかへ　おでかけでしたか。
(Did you go out yesterday? *lit.* — Did you go somewhere yesterday?)

Mr. Lerner understood that this just meant "I hope you had a good weekend," but he suddenly realized that Mr. Okada often uses *o ... desu* or *o ... deshita,* expressions which he himself does not use very often.

* * *

Odekake-ni narimashita-ka is correct and polite, but *... ni narimashita-ka* is often replaced by *o ... deshita-ka* in conversation because it sounds less direct and more refined. For example, it sounds more refined to say

Okaeri-desu-ka
than
Okaeri-ni narimasu-ka

when asking whether the other person is leaving.
In the same way, *... ni irasshaimasu-ka* can also be replaced by *... desu-ka,* as in

Okusan-wa otaku-desu-ka.

meaning *Okusan-wa otaku-ni irasshaimasu-ka.* (Is your wife home?)
Sometimes even longer phrases can be replaced by *... desu-ka* as in

Ojoosan-wa chuugaku-desu-ka.

meaning *Ojoosan-wa chuugaku-ni itte-irasshaimasu-ka.* (Does your daughter go to middle school?)

When asking someone about what he did in the past, . . . *deshita-ka* is used as in

Yuube-wa nanji-goro okaeri-deshita-ka.
(What time did you return home last night?)

Sometimes . . . *deshoo-ka* is used in the same way as in

Sensee-wa moo okaeri-deshoo-ka.
(Is the professor home now?)

This pattern is used with many verbs, especially those that are commonly used in social situations, as in

Nagaku omachi-desu-ka.
(Have you been waiting for long?)
Donata-o osagashi-desu-ka.
(Whom are you looking for?)
Donataka otazune-desu-ka.
(Have you come to visit someone?)

. . . no koto-desu-ga
used when starting a statement

When Mr. Lerner went to ask Miss Yoshida about something, Mr. Takada had just come up to talk to her. He first said *Anoo . . .* and after she answered *Hai,* he said

Kinoo tanonda shorui-no koto-da-kedo.
(*lit.* It's about the papers I asked you to help me with yesterday.)

She answered *Ee,* and he said

Moo dekiteru? (Are they ready?)

Mr. Lerner did not talk in this way but used one sentence instead, as in *Kinoo tanonda shorui-wa dekite-imasu-ka.* He wondered if this was inappropriate.

*　　　*　　　*

When making a request, it is common to use some preliminary remark before actually stating the request, as in

Sumimasen-kedo, chotto tetsudatte-kudasaimasen-ka.
(I'm sorry to trouble you, but could you help me?)
Warui-kedo, kore, naoshite-kurenai?
(Sorry to trouble you, but will you repair this for me?)

to avoid sounding abrupt. But this is not limited to the case of requests. When asking a question or even when giving information as well, it is highly regarded in Japanese conversation to make some preliminary remark before actually stating what one wants to say.

Suppose you go to someone where he or she is working and ask if something is ready. It is all right to talk like this: you will first say

Anoo . . . (1)

and after the listener has said Hai, you will say

Kinoo tanonda kopii, dekite-imasu-ka. (2)
(Have you finished the copying I asked you to do yesterday?)

In this way you have used two steps. However, if you use three steps instead, it will sound more reserved. Namely,

(1) Speaker: Anoo . . .
    Listener: Hai.
(2) Speaker: Kinoo tanonda kopii-no koto-desu-ga.
    Listener: Hai.
(3) Moo dekite-imasu-ka.

Politeness is indicated not only by polite wording but also by using a greater number of these steps. In other words, if someone is merely verbally polite but uses too few steps, it sounds impolite. If someone said Makoto-ni osoreirimasu-ga kono shorui-o kopii-shite-kudasaimasen-ka in one breath — namely in one step, it would not sound polite even though the words themselves are polite.

Some words used for counting things

When he met Miss Yoshida on Monday morning, Mr. Lerner wanted to tell her that he had seen a couple of movies over the weekend. He said

Shuumatsu-ni nihon-no eega-o mimashita.

meaning "I saw two movies over the weekend." Miss Yoshida looked rather surprised and said something admiring. After further discussion he realized that she thought that he had seen Japanese movies. Everybody at the office was amused at this misunderstanding — namely taking *nihon-no* (two) for *nihon-no* (Japanese).

*   *   *

This misunderstanding was caused by two things. One was a mistake in accent. To mean "two movies" he should have said

   ni
     ho n no   二本の

instead of saying

     ho n no   日本の
   ni

The latter accent pattern is used for the word *nihon-no* (of Japan), as in *nihon-no hana* (Japanese flowers) and *nihon-no josee* (Japanese women).

The other reason concerns the use of *nihon*. The counter *hon* is used for counting long, thin objects like needles, pencils, pillars and cigarettes. It is also used for films and tapes because they are long and thin. Mr. Lerner was right in using *hon* for counting movies, but he should have said

Eega-o nihon mimashita.

rather than

Nihon-no eega-o mimashita.

It is more common in conversation to say the number after the name of the thing. Thus *nisatsu-no hon* (two books) will be understood but it is more conversational to say

Hon-o nisatsu yomimashita.

In the same way, it is more common to say things like

Okane-o sen-en haraimashita.
(I paid 1,000 yen.)
Koohii-o nihai nomimashita.
(I drank two cups of coffee.)
Negi-o sanbon kudasai.
(Please give me three *negi* — Japanese leek.)

than saying *sen-en-no okane, nihai-no koohii* or *sanbon-no negi.*

Signals to indicate that one is going to start talking

When Mr. Lerner was walking along the hall in the office, he saw Mr. Okada coming from the other direction. Before he could start saying *Konnichiwa*, Mr. Okada first said

A, Raanaa-san, doomo.
あ、ラーナーさん、どうも。
(Hi, Mr. Lerner.)

It was just a short phrase, but he suddenly realized that most Japanese say *A!* before saying *Konnichiwa* or *Ohayoo-gozaimasu* when they meet. It seemed to him as if these sounds were used as an opening quotation mark. He wondered if this was necessary or just personal preference.

* * *

When two people meet on the street or in the hall, come to a certain distance from each other, and start greeting each other, it can be observed that in most cases they first give some short sound like *A!* or *Ha!* This is especially true when the two people are not on intimate terms, or when they are talking politely.

The Japanese regard it, whether consciously or unconsciously, as appropriate to give some signal to show that they are going to start talking. If they hear someone say *Yamamoto-san!* to them all of a sudden, they will feel somewhat alarmed. This often happens when talking with foreigners; when they recognize their acquaintances, most foreigners say *Konnichiwa* or *Yamamoto-san* immediately without giving such signals. This seems the same to the Japanese as opening a door without knocking. Opening the door without knocking is permissible in the case of children or between family members or good friends in Japan; in the same way, children usually do not give this verbal signal and family members and good friends do not use it either. Only in polite situations does one have to give such a signal.

Sometimes bowing slightly takes the place of giving a verbal signal. What counts most is to give a certain signal before starting to talk.

The notorious Japanese custom of sharply inhaling or sucking teeth during speech also serves the same purpose. This is done in formal and polite speech, mainly by men; it shows that the speaker feels it necessary to give a special signal before daring to talk to someone he respects very much.

The first part of a sentence implying the rest

Mr. Lerner was riding in Miss Yoshida's car last Saturday. When she turned on the car radio, the news had already started. The announcer said

Sakuya juuji-goro
(Last night, about 10 o'clock)

then gave the place name and started saying

... *chuunen-no otoko-ga* ...　……中年の男が……
(... a middle-aged man ...)

Then Miss Yoshida suddenly changed the channel. When Mr. Lerner asked her why, she said that she knew it was about some disgraceful crime and she did not care to listen to it. He wondered how the first phrase *chuunen-no otoko-ga* was enough to indicate the nature of the news.

*　　　*　　　*

Miss Yoshida was right. If a news item starts with *chuunen-no otoko*, it is definitely about some disgraceful crime. The word *otoko* does not imply respect and cannot be used with someone worthy of respect. The same thing applies to the word *onna*. To refer to a person without any derogatory connotation in formal or polite speech, one either has to add *hito* as in

otoko-no-hito
or
onna-no-hito
or use other words such as
dansee (man)
or

josee (woman).

If the news is about a man who is a victim, not a criminal, the announcer will say *otoko-no-hito* or something like *gojissai-gurai-no otoko-no-hito* (a man about 50 years old). The word *otoko* by itself sounds denigrating when used in public reporting and *chuunen-no* makes the implication even worse.

The listener to a newscast can judge whether what will follow is about a praiseworthy event or a disgraceful one just by listening to the first part — namely, whether *otoko* or *otoko-no-hito* is used. In the same way, while listening to someone talking, one constantly anticipates what kind of statement will follow, and this makes listening easier. A native speaker of a language can be relaxed in listening because to some extent he can anticipate what will come next. Therefore it is important, when learning a foreign language, to learn words or phrases in their appropriate context.

Haitte-iru vs. *irete-aru*

When Mr. Lerner was looking for a document a few days ago and asked Miss Yoshida about it, she said, while pointing to one of the cabinets,

Asoko-ni irete-arimasu. (It's in there.)

But today, when Mr. Takada asked her about something else, she said, while looking into one of the cabinets,

Aa, koko-ni haitte-imasu. (It's in here.)

Mr. Lerner had learned that *irete-arimasu* and *haitte-imasu* are used to refer to the same situation; he wondered if there is any difference in the speaker's attitude in the two expressions.

*   *   *

To describe a state, two expressions can be used; one is to add *te-iru* to intransitive verbs and the other is to add *te-aru* to transitive verbs. Namely, *aite-imasu* and *akete-arimasu* both mean "the door is open," and *shimatte-imasu* and *shimete-arimasu* both refer to something being closed.

あいています／あけてあります
しまっています／しめてあります

Although the situation which is referred to by the two types of expressions is the same, the speaker's attitude is different. When the speaker wants to describe a situation as it is, without considering who caused it to be so, . . . *te-imasu* is used. When the speaker is conscious of someone having done something to cause the state, he uses . . . *te-*

arimasu. Thus saying *Mado-ga akete-arimasu* implies "Someone has opened it so that it is now open." At finding a lock broken, one will use *Kagi-ga kowarete-imasu* to report the condition and *Kagi-ga kowashite-arimasu* to imply that someone has intentionally broken it.

Sometimes the speaker uses . . . *te-aru* to imply that someone is responsible for the situation, in many cases implying that he himself did it with good intentions. Miss Yoshida may have said *irete-arimasu* to imply that she placed the document there herself. When she said *haitte-imasu,* she was not interested in who placed it there.

When a husband asks his wife if the bath is ready, she may say either

Ee, waite-imasu.

or

Ee, wakashite-arimasu.

Both mean "Yes, it's heated," but the second one implies that she did it for her husband. If she wants to emphasize her having done it for him, she will say

Ee, wakashite-okimashita.

Sore-de vs. *sore-dewa*

Mr. Lerner was telling his colleagues about what had happened to him over the weekend. He took Mr. Okada to a restaurant, but when he went to pay, he found that he had left his wallet at home. He told them this, and added

Sore-dewa Okada-san-ni karimashita.

meaning "So I borrowed some money from Mr. Okada." Everybody understood him but Miss Yoshida remarked that he should have used *sore-de* instead of *sore-dewa*. He wondered if adding *wa* makes much difference in meaning.

*   *   *

Yes, it does. While *sore-de* is used when one continues one's own speech, *sore-dewa* is used when one starts talking about something else. Thus, when one has said

Saifu-o wasurete kimashita. Sore-de . . .

one adds such phrases as

   . . . *Okada-san-ni karimashita.*
   (I borrowed money from Mr. Okada.)
   . . . *uchi-e tori-ni kaerimashita.*
   (I went back home to get it.)

On the other hand, *sore-dewa* is used by the listener as in

  A: *Saifu-o wasurete-kimashita.*
  B: *Sore-dewa kore-o otsukai-kudasai.*
  (Then, please use this money.)

or,

    A: *Saifu-o wasure-mashita.*
    B: *Sore-dewa komatta-deshoo.*
(Then you must have been embarrassed.)

Although *sore-de* is used to continue one's own speech, the other person sometimes uses it for the same purpose as in:

    A: *Saifu-o wasurete-kimashita.*
    B: *Sore-de . . .*
    A: *Sore-de Okada-san-ni karimashita.*

The other person is helping the speaker to go on. In this case, the listener is participating in completing the speaker's sentence, rather than starting a sentence of his own.

Negation of a reason

Recently Mr. Lerner has been going drinking with his colleagues after work. Hearing that he planned to go yesterday evening too, Miss Yoshida teased him saying that he had started acting like a Japanese businessman. So he also replied jokingly

Suki-da-kara nomimasen.

meaning "I don't drink because I like to." Miss Yoshida understood, but said that it sounded strange somehow.

           *   *   *

To indicate that one drinks but the reason is not that one likes to drink, one can also say something like

Nomimasu-keredomo, hontoo-wa suki-ja arimasen.
(I drink all right, but I don't really like drinking.)

But Mr. Lerner tried to use a more compact and advanced expression, and did not use it exactly right.

Saying *Suki-da-kara nomimasen* sounds strange, because the last part *nomimasen* means "I don't drink." The whole thing in English would be, if literally translated, "Because I like it, I don't drink."

He should have said

Suki-da-kara nomu-n-ja arimasen.
(*lit.* It is not that I drink because I like it.)
or
Suki-da-kara nomu wake-ja arimasen.

138

(*lit.* The situation is not that I drink because I like it.)

To deny a reason for doing something, the basic pattern is to add

... *-n (o)-ja arimasen* or ... *wake-ja arimasen.*

You may have heard the Japanese use such expressions as follow.

Gekkyuu-ga yasui-kara yameta wake-ja arimasen. Shigoto-ga awanai-kara-desu.
(I didn't quit my job because the pay was low. The work did not suit me.)

Atama-ga warukute shippai-shita-n-ja arimasen. Un-ga warukatta-n-desu.
(He didn't fail because he was not smart enough. He was unlucky.)

Pittari, sutto, etc. —
the use of mimicry words

Mr. Takada was working hard on some figures yesterday evening when most of his colleagues were starting to leave the office. Mr. Lerner and Miss Yoshida were waiting for him to finish his work so that they could go together to have some tea. Suddenly Mr. Takada said

Aa, pittari-da. Sutto shita.　ぴったり　すっと

Mr. Lerner did not understand, but Miss Yoshida joyfully said

Soo. Ja, satto demashoo-yo.　さっと

He understood that she was proposing they leave at once, but he wondered what these onomatopoeic words meant.

*　　　*　　　*

Mr. Takada said *pittari-da* to mean that the figures coincided exactly. He was happy that he found the calculations to be correct. The word *pittari* describes two things matching or agreeing completely, as in

Futari-no iken-ga pittari atta.
(The opinions of the two agreed exactly.)
Kono neji, pittari hamarimashita-yo.
(This screw fits exactly.)

One might say *kanzen-ni* (completely), but saying *pittari* describes the situation more vividly.

By saying *sutto shita,* Mr. Takada meant that he was quite relieved and happy. *Sutto* is used to describe something quickly going off; *sutto shita*

140

indicates that what had been worrying Mr. Takada was suddenly resolved. And Miss Yoshida said *satto demashoo-yo* meaning "let's go out quickly." *Satto* describes a quick action; it is often used when people leave quickly as in

Jugyoo-ga owaru-to gakusee-wa satto inaku natta.
(The students left the moment the class was over.)

This word too can be replaced by *hayaku* or *sugu*, but *satto* is often preferred as being the more lively description.

Words describing sound or action directly and vividly are called onomatopoeic words or mimicry words. For instance, *batan* describes the sound of a door closing just like the English "to bang shut," and *zaazaa* describes rain falling hard. Such words as *pittari, sutto* and *satto* are also called mimicry words. Onomatopoeic or mimicry words have a fairly high position in Japanese. They are not regarded as children's words; adults also use them often in daily conversation. In addition, they are frequently used in the works of famous novelists and poets.

The intonation of *Soo-desu-ka*

Mr. Lerner can now make himself understood in Japanese and is improving in his vocabulary and grammar, but he still has some problems with his intonation. Just this morning, when Mr. Mori, the director of the company, remarked that his golf game had improved recently, he said

Soo-desu-ka. (Is that so?)

It was a very simple sentence, but it seemed to be unpleasant to Mr. Mori. Miss Yoshida, who was with them, later told Mr. Lerner that the tone had sounded impolite because he had raised the last *ka* sound.

*　　　*　　　*

To make a sentence a question, *ka* is usually added, as in

Oisogashii-desu-ka. (Are you busy?)

This *ka* is said with a higher pitch than *desu* as in

So　　　*-ka?*
　　o-desu

How high the *ka* is said depends on the speaker's intention. When he is anxious to know the answer he raises the *ka* very high. Otherwise *ka* should not be raised too high. And foreigners are advised not to keep going up as in

```
          -ka?
       su
    -de
      o
   So
```

Just the last *ka* should be raised.

Sentences ending with *ka*, however, do not always indicate a question. Just like the English "Is that right?", *Soo-desu-ka* is often said as an answer. When it is used as an answer, the last *ka* should not go up.

Such sentences should be said as in

```
   So
      o-desu-ka.
```

If the *ka* goes up, it implies that the speaker has doubts. Mr. Lerner probably unconsciously used this intonation, which sounded impolite. Especially when the *ka* is said long and raised as in

```
              a?
   So       -ka
     o-desu
```

it definitely indicates distrust.

Ne as in *Soo-desu-ne* and *yo* as in *Soo-desu-yo* are also said either with a falling intonation or a rising one, depending on the speaker's intention. *Ne* is said high when one solicits agreement, and is raised higher to indicate warmth or anxiousness. *Yo* is usually said with a falling tone; if you raise it, it will sound as if you are talking to a child.

Tomo and *mochiron* used for emphasis

Mr. Lerner was awaiting his turn at the dentist's yesterday afternoon. He wanted to smoke, so asked the old woman sitting next to him

Tabako, sutte-mo kamaimasen-ka.
(Would you mind if I smoked?)

The old woman looked a little surprised, and then said hurriedly

Ee, ee, kamaimasen-tomo. Doozo, doozo.
(Oh, not at all. Please go ahead.)

Mr. Lerner could not hear exactly what she added to *kamaimasen*. Later he learned from Miss Yoshida that *tomo* is used for emphasis, and wondered if he could use it himself.

*　　　*　　　*

Tomo is added for emphasis as in

Kekkoo-desu-tomo.
(It's perfectly fine with me.)
Ma-ni aimasu-tomo.
(You will certainly be in time.)

It can be used in familiar conversation too, as in

Ii-tomo. (Okay!)

This ending is used more often by fairly old people now, and when young people use it, it sounds rather dramatic. Young people usually use *yo* for emphasis rather than *tomo*.

To show emphasis when granting someone's

request, one also uses *mochiron* (of course) as in

> *Ee, mochiron kamaimasen.*
> (I don't mind it at all.)
> *Mochiron ma-ni aimasu.*
> (Of course you will be in time.)

Sometimes both *mochiron* and *tomo* are used together as in

> *Ee, mochiron kamaimasen-tomo.*

But one should be careful when using *mochiron* in answer to a question, instead of a request, in polite conversation. When asked something like

> *Nihongo owakari-desu-ka.*
> (Do you understand Japanese?)

saying *Mochiron* can imply that the question is either silly or insulting. You should simply say *Hai* or *Ee, wakarimasu.*

Ohiru-demo tabemashoo-ka —
Indirect expressions

Mr. Okada came to discuss some business with Mr. Lerner and Mr. Takada yesterday morning. When the discussions were finished it was almost noon. Mr. Takada said.

Ja, ohiru-demo tabemashoo-ka.
じゃ、 おひるでも　たべましょうか。

and the two agreed and went out. Mr. Lerner had heard the expression *Ocha-demo nomimashoo-ka* (Shall we have tea or something like that?) and now realized that this *demo* (or something like that) can be used with *ohiru* (lunch), too.

*　　　*　　　*

The Japanese often use an indirect form of expression when making requests or proposals in social situation. They prefer saying

Doo-desu-ka. Ocha-demo nomimasen-ka.
(What about having tea or something like that?)

to saying . . . *ocha-o nomimasen-ka,* which sounds more direct. The use of *demo* implies that the speaker does not want to press the listener with a definite proposal and wants to let the listener choose what he likes among several possibilities. Thus *demo* is often used to show the speaker's consideration toward the listener when making suggestions as in

Terebi-demo mimashoo-ka.
(Shall we watch TV?)

146

Sanpo-demo shimasen-ka.
(What about taking a walk?)

When one says *Ohiru-demo tabemashoo-ka* (Shall we have lunch?), however, he does not have any definite alternative to lunch in mind. In fact, what else would one do other than have lunch when one goes out at lunchtime? In this case *demo* is used simply to make the phrasing less direct and thus show consideration toward the listener.

This type of indirect expression is used most often in social situations, but sometimes it is used even when one does not have to show consideration to the listener, such as when talking to oneself. For instance, one might say, while leaving his desk on a coffee break,

Saa, te-demo araoo-ka.
(Well, I might as well wash my hands.)

Some people like using such indirect expressions because they imply that the speaker has freedom in choosing what to do and is not acting according to an immediate necessity or someone else's orders.

Ka used to show reserve

Yesterday afternoon Mr. Lerner discussed some business with Mr. Okada. When the discussions were over, and they were deciding on their next meeting, Mr. Okada said

Kono hi-ga ii-ka-to omoimasu.
(I think this day might be good.)

Mr. Lerner noticed that he inserted *ka* between *ii* and *to omoimasu*; he understood that this *ka* indicates uncertainty, but he had not paid much attention to it before. After he started listening for it, he realized that this *ka* is used very often.

*　　　*　　　*

Ka is used to indicate either that one is uncertain about the matter or to make the statement less direct. It can be added to various words and phrases. As in Mr. Okada's statement, it is often added to adjectives as in

Mada hayai-ka-to omoimasu.
まだ　早いかと　おもいます。
(I'm afraid it is too early yet.)
Chotto takai-ka-to omoimasu.
(I'm afraid it is a little expensive.)

It can be added to verbs as in

Ashita-wa kuru-ka-to omoimasu.
(I think he will come tomorrow.)
Mada ma-ni au-ka-to omoimasu.
(I think I will be in time.)

And even nouns can be followed by this *ka* as in

Moo jikan-ka-to omoimasu.
(I think it is about time now.)
Choodo ichiman-en-ka-to omoimasu.
(I think it is exactly 10,000 yen.)

These examples sound rather polite, but this *ka* can be used in non-polite speech too, as in

Sore-de ii-ka-to omou-kedo, moo ichido kangaete-miyoo.
(I think it's all right, but I will think about it again.)

The expression ... *n-ja nai-ka-to omoimasu* is used in a similar way; this sounds more informal and is used very often.

When one has to show reserve in social situations, ... *ka-to omoimasu* is used. For instance, when a company worker wants to remind his boss that it is time to start doing something, it would sound too direct and blunt to say

Moo jikan-da-to omoimasu.

He will normally use such expression as

Moo jikan-ka-to omoimasu.

or, to sound more reserved,

Ano, sorosoro jikan-ka-to omoimasu-ga.

The difference between *sono* and *ano*

Mr. Lerner wanted to be excused from the office for a few hours yesterday afternoon because a friend of his was coming to Japan and he had to go to the airport to meet him. He explained to Mr. Mori, the director, that his friend was coming and added,

Ano tomodachi-wa Nihon-e hajimete kimasu.
(This is the first visit to Japan for that friend of mine.)

Mr. Mori said it was all right for him to go, but Miss Yoshida, who was with them, later told him that he should have used *sono* instead of *ano*.

*　　　*　　　*

To refer to something physically close to the speaker, *kono* or *kore* is used; to refer to something close to the listener *sore* or *sono* is used, and something far from both the speaker and listener is referred to with *are* or *ano*.

However, when you refer to something non-physical, different rules apply. When you refer to someone or something that the listener knows, you use *ano,* and otherwise you use *sono*. (*Kono* is used when you want to emphatically refer to it.) If the listener knows the person you are referring to, you say

Kinoo Yamada-san-ni aimashita. Ano-hito, genki-deshita-yo.
(I met Mr. Yamada yesterday. He was very fine.)

But when the listener has not met Mr. Yamada, you

have to say

> *Kinoo Yamada-to yuu hito-ni aimashita. Sono-hito-wa daigaku-no toki-no tomodachi-desu-ga . . .*
>
> (I met a Mr. Yamada yesterday. He is my friend from university days.)

Since Mr. Mori does not know Mr. Lerner's friend, Mr. Lerner should have said *sono tomodachi* instead of *ano tomodachi*.

Sometimes one forgets that the listener has not met the person, and in such cases the conversation will be as follows:

> A: *Kinoo Yamada-san-ni aimashita.*
>
> B: *Haa . . .*
>
> A: *Ano-hito genki-deshita-yo.*
>
> A: *Ano-hito-tte, watashi mada atte-nai-to omoimasu-ga.*
>
> A: *Soo-soo. Shitsuree-shimashita.*
>
> (A: I met Mr. Yamada yesterday. B: Oh? A: He was very fine. B: Mr. Yamada . . . I believe I haven't met him yet. A: That's right. Excuse me.)

Expressions indicating the subject

Yesterday afternoon when Mr. Lerner went to talk to Ms. Yoshida about a work matter, she looked a little upset. She explained that she had misplaced some important papers and was looking for them, and then she added

Watashi-tte honto-ni dame-desu-ne.
(*lit.* I'm really bad.)

almost talking to herself. The papers were soon found and her worry was over, but Mr. Lerner wondered if this *tte* is used to indicate the subject of a sentence, as *wa* is.

* * *

To describe how a person or a thing is, usually *wa* is used as in

Ano-hito-wa shinsetsuna hito-desu.
(She is a kind person.)
Kono shigoto-wa jikan-ga kakarimasu.
(This work takes a lot of time.)

Ms. Yoshida could have said

Watashi-wa honto-ni dame-desu-ne.

too. The difference is that *tte* is more emphatic. This is an abbreviation of . . . *to yuu mono-wa* or . . . *to yuu koto-wa* (what is called. . .). The speaker indicates his emotion when he uses *tte* instead of *wa*. Saying

Ano-hito-tte shinsetsuna hito-desu-ne.

sounds more emphatic. In the same way you can also say

> *Onna-ga shigoto-suru-tte taihenna koto-desu.*
> (It is rough for a woman to work.)

When *tte* is used after a verb, it should be paraphrased as ... *to yuu koto-wa.*

Several other words are also used to indicate the subject.

Tara is one of them. It also reflects the speaker's emotion, usually one of surprise or disapproval, as in

> *Yamada-san-tara, kyoo-wa hen-desu-ne.*
> (Mr. Yamada is acting strangely today.)

When the subject is given as a representative of similar things, *nanka* is used as in

> *Yamada-san-nanka dame-desu-yo.*
> (People like Mr. Yamada are no good.)

In fact, various words other than *wa* or *ga* are used to indicate the subject. And when there is no need of emphasis very often nothing is added to the subject, as in

> *Watashi, dame-desu-ne.*
> *Ano-hito, shinsetsuna hito-desu-ne.*
> *Yamada-san, kyoo-wa hen-desu-ne.*

Leaving *wa* out in this way is not regarded as sloppy speech. In fact, this can be done in polite speech, too.

Common sayings and fixed numbers of syllables

While Mr. Lerner and Miss Yoshida were walking along the street after lunch, he noticed a signboard saying

Tobidasu-na, kuruma-wa kyuu-ni tomarenai.
(Don't run out; cars cannot stop immediately.)

This was all written in *hiragana;* he happened to count the number of syllables and found that it consisted of 17 syllables. He remarked to Miss Yoshida that it was like *haiku,* a form of traditional poem. She smiled and gave another example:

Kagi kakete, otonari-san-ni koe kakete.
(Lock the door and tell your neighbor you're going out.)

*　　　*　　　*

Syllables in Japanese are pronounced with approximately the same length, and the numbers of syllables are important in forming rhythm. Traditionally most Japanese poem forms use phrases of either 5 or 7 syllables. *Waka* or *tanka* consists of 5 lines — 5, 7, 5, 7, 7, and *haiku* of 3 lines — 5, 7, 5. Among present-day songs too, many lines consist of either 5 or 7 syllables. Even when making up the sayings for various campaigns the Japanese prefer phrases of 5 or 7 syllables.

The two sayings mentioned above were recently devised by public agencies to warn people against danger, traffic and criminals. The first one consists of 17 syllables; *tobidasu-na* (don't run out) has 5 syllables, *kuruma-wa kyuu-ni* (cars immediately) 7, and *tomarenai* (can't stop) 5. The second one also has 17 syllables; *kagi kakete* (lock up)

5, *otonari-san-ni* (to your neighbor) 7, and *koe kakete* (speak to) 5. In addition, this makes use of a pun; *kakeru* is used twice; *kagi-o kakeru* means "to lock," and *koe-o kakeru* means "to speak to someone." Usually *o* is added to *kagi* (key) and *koe* (voice), but here it is left out in order to make the phrases 5 syllables long.

Just recently a newspaper reported that a group of people were seen cleaning the streets of Tokyo with a sash across their chests reading

Otto mate, sono gomi chan-to kuzukago-e.

(Hey, wait. Put that trash into the trash can where it belongs.)

This phrase also consists of 17 syllables; *irete-kudasai* (please put it) is understood and left out after *kuzukago-e* (into the trash can).

INDEX TO WORDS, PHRASES AND SENTENCES Vol. 6

A

accent	128
aizuchi	81
anna	150-1
ano	150-1
apology about previous meetings	12-3
. . . areru (respect)	66-7
ariawase	51
Arigatoo-gozaimashita.	38
arya	68
asking for instructions	58-9
asking someone's wishes politely	59
asking someone to return a phone call	32-3
attributing the merit to someone else	91

B

bai-bai	15
batan	141
being hurt in a fall	48-9
belittling one's gift	30-1
bowing	8-9, 80, 131
burabura-suru	93

C

calling a waitress' attention	23
calling just before one's visit	24
changes in the meaning of words	64-5
chan-to	88-9
chef's recommendation	23
Chotto . . .	22
Chotto sono hen-made mairimashita-node.	24
chuunen-no otoko	132
classroom Japanese	58, 59
common sayings	154-5
completing someone's unfinished statement	81
compliments	11
compliment on a foreigner's Japanese	42
context	133
contracted forms	106-7
conversation opening	10-1, 42
conveying a message	34-5, 82-3

D

dangling tone	69

A (second column)

. . . dasu	112-3
. . . dasu vs. . . . hajimeru .	112-3
De, kyoo-wa . . .	20
declining an offer of help ...	36-7
denial, strong	116-7
-demo	146-7
describing being hurt in a fall	48-9
describing headade	46-7
describing stomachache	44-5
(o) . . . deshita-ka	124-5
(o) . . . deshoo-ka	125
(o) . . . desu-ka	124-5
desu-mono	96-7
Dewa, kore-de.	16
Dewa, kore-de shitsuree-shimasu.	25
different attitude in the speaker's part	76-7
doo . . . eba ii-deshoo	58-9
doo-yuu	157
Doozo yoroshiku.	8
doshindoshin	46
doshidoshi	46

E

end of business discussions	18-9
evaluation	89
expectations	88-9
expressions indicating the subject	152-3
expressions meaning "as you know"	40-1
expressions meaning "not all . . ."	114-5
expressions meaning "please accept it"	30
expressions of apology or gratitude about previous meetings	12-3
expressions of gratitude and compliments	11
expressions of pleasure	90-1
expressions used at the end of business discussions ...	18-9
expressions used for strong denial	116-7
expressions used when starting a statement	126-7

F

family language	97
first part of a sentence implying the rest	132-3

G

. . . (desu)-ga 68-9
(noun, pronoun)-ga 153
gangan 47
giving directions 56-7
giving someone's name
  without any terms of
  respect 29
Gokigen-yoo. 15
Gokuroosama. 63
Gomen-kudasai(-mase). 15, 19
goran-ni naru 120-1
Gozonji-desu-ka. 40
gratitude about previous
  meetings 12-3
gratitude for help 38-9

H

haiku 154
haitte-iru vs. irete-aru 134-5
hakkiri shinai 47
hanashikakeru 118-9
hanashikomu 123
hazu-ga nai 116
headache, description of 46-7
higamu 111
hirihiri 49
-hon (counter) 128-9
honno 50-1
Honno kimochi-desu. 50-1
hyotto suru-to 94

I

ii tokoro 100-1
Iie, kekkoo-desu. 36
Iie, koko-de shitsuree-
  shimasu. 24
iku toki vs. itta toki 75
indirect expressions 146-7
Itte-mairimasu. 16-7
Itte-rasshai. 16-7

J

Ja. 14,19,63
Ja, ato-de. 16
Ja, kore-de shitsuree-
  shimasu. 17
Ja, mata. 14, 63
Ja, sonna tokoro-de. 18
Jitsu-wa 20-1

K

ka in Soo-desu-ka 142-3
ka used to show reserve 148-9
kaeru toki vs. kaetta toki 74-5
. . . kakeru 119

kamo shirenai 94
kanai vs. tsuma 28
kanji compounds 67
kara 26-7
keredomo 68-9
. . . kirenai 115
kirikiri 44, 46
. . . kko nai 116-7
kochira 108
Kochira-koso. 8
Kochira-koso totsuzen
  ojama-shimashite. 25
Kochira . . . desu. 8
. . . komu 122-3
kono 150-1
kore 150-1
korobu 48
korya 68
koto used to mean
  "necessity" 98-9
koto-ni yoru-to 94
kotozuke 32
kudasaru 53
kureru 53
kuru hito vs. kita hito 75

L

leaving a message 32-3
listener anticipating what
  will come next 133
listener participating in
  completing the speaker's
  sentence 137

M

mada . . . te-inai 70-1
Maido arigatoo-gozaimasu. .. 62
making a request in a
  reserved way 26-7
making explanations 40-1
Makoto-ni tsumaranai mono-
  desu-ga. 30
. . . mase 120
. . . mashita 70
. . . mashite 81
. . . masu vs. . . . te-
  kudasai used for giving
  directions 56-7
meeshi 9
mimicry words 140-1
minshuku 62
mochiron 144-5
mon(o)-desu-ka 116
. . . mon(o)-ka 116
moo sukoshi-de . . . suru
  tokoro-datta 101
moshika-shitara 94-5
moshika-suru-to 94-5

N

. . . *n-ja arimasen* 138-9
. . .*n-ja nai-ka-to omoimasu* 149
na used for a familiar
  command 84-5
na used for negative
  imperative 82-3
name card 9
. . . *nanka* 153
nantoka . . . dekiru 37
. . . *nasai*........................ 84, 120-1
ne 143
negation of a reason 138-9
negative imperative 82
nihon-no (two) 128-9
. . . *niwa osewa-ni natte-*
  orimasu 10
. . . *no koto-desu-ga* 126-7
node 26-7
nonbiri-suru 93
noni 76-7
noni vs. *keredomo* 76-7
"not all . . ." 114-5
number of syllables 154-5

O

Ojikan-o torimashite. 19
Okaerinasai. 120
Ocha-mo sashiagemasen-
  de. 25
okage 43
Okagesama-de. 39
Onegai-(ita)shimasu. 23, 38
onna vs. *onna-no-hito* 132
onomatopoeic words 140-1
orusu-ni 34
Osaki-ni (shitsuree-
  shimasu). 14-5
Osewasama. 63
oshikomu 122-3
Osoreirimasu. 38
Otaku-kara denwa-desu. 29
otoko vs. *otoko-no-hito* 132
Otsukaresama..................... 14, 62-3
Oyasuminasai. 120
oyobitate 19

P

passive form 54
physical distance between
  the speakers 8
pittari 140-1
plain imperative 82
"please accept it" 30
pleasure, expressions of 90-1
position of phrases
  indicating numbers 129

. . . *ppoi* 110-1
preliminary remarks 126-7
pronunciation making the
  meaning clear 107
process of receiving a gift .. 30-1
pun 155

R

redundancy 60-1
refusal 31,36
repeated expression of
  gratitude or apology 13
repeating similar
  expressions 19
responding to a
  compliment 42-3
rhetorical question 116-7

S

sareru 66-7
sakihodo-wa 13
satto 140-1
sayonara........................... 14-5, 16, 19
sekkaku . . . noni 77
self-defense 96
Senjitsu-wa gochisoosama-
  deshita. 12
sentence subject 152-3
sharply inhaling or sucking
  teeth during speech 131
shikushiku 44
Shitte-imasu-ka. 40
shitsuree-shimasu 15, 19
signals to show the start of
  business discussions 20
signals to show that one is
  going to start talking 130
signs and written
  instructions 83
sochira 108-9
something that the speaker
  cannot control 72-3
sonna................................ 117
sono 150-1
sono vs. *ano* 150-1
. . . *soo-desu* 34-5
soo-desu-ka, intonation of ... 142-3
soo-yuu koto-de 18
sore 150-1
sore-de vs. *sore-dewa* 136-7
Sore-ja, yoroshiku. 18
sore-wa 68
sorya 68-9
soryaa 68-9
sounding hesitant or
  apologetic when making a
  request 27

speaker and listener
  participating in a flow of
  speech 81
speaker's attitude 134-5
speaker's will 72-3
stem plus -wa shinai 106-7
starting a statement 126-7
stomachache, description
  of 44-5
suffering from someone's
  actions 54-5
Sumimasen-deshita. 39
surimuku 49
. . . suru koto-ga aru 98-9
. . . suru koto-ni naru 98-9
. . . suru koto-ni suru 98-9
suru used to mean "to
  cost" 92-3
sutto 140-1

T

ta form 38-9
. . . ta bakari 47
. . . ta koto-ga aru 98-9
. . . ta tokoro-de 101
ta used to indicate the
  completion of an action ... 74-5
tabena vs. taberu-na 84
tabun 94-5
taishita 37
tanka 154
taoreru 48
. . . tara 153
Tasukarimashita. 19, 39
tazunete-kuru 52-3
thanking someone for his
  kindness to one's family
  member 11
thinking in kanji 65
. . . te used to end a
  sentence 80-1
. . . te used to indicate a
  reason 72-3
. . . te vs. . . . node, . . .
  kara 73
. . . te-imasen 70-1
. . . te-imasen vs. . . .
  masen-deshita 70-1
. . . te-iru vs. . . . te-aru 134-5
. . . te-itadaku 104-5
. . . te-iru tokoro 101
. . . te-kureru 53
. . . te-kuru...................... 52-3, 113
. . . te-ne......................... 80-1, 85
. . . te-oku 135
. . . te-wa ikemasen 83, 87
. . . te-wa komarimasu 87
. . . te-wa used to indicate

condition 86-7
. . . te-wa vs. . . . eba 86-7
. . . to osshaimashita 35
. . . tokoro made-wa ikanai . 115
tokoro used to mean
  "situation" 100-1
tomo 144-5
tone and the speaker's
  intention 69
. . . tte............................ 35, 82-3
. . . tte vs. . . . wa 152-3
Totsuzen
  ojama-itashimashite. 25
tsuma 28
tsure 22

U

ureshii 90-1
using greater number of
  steps 127

V

verbal politeness............ 104-5,127
visiting someone without
  notice 24

W

wa, leaving out 153
wa used to mean "not
  all . . ." 114-5
wa vs. ga 78-9
. . . wa shitsuree-
  shimashita 13
waka 153
. . . wake-ja arimasen..... 115, 138-9
Warui(-ne, -wane). 38
warui tokoro 101
Warukatta(-ne, -wane). 39
watashi-ga vs. watashi-wa ... 78-9
wife reporting her
  husband's absence from
  the office 29

Y

yo added to . . . na 84
yoroshiku 90
yoyaku 60
yukkuri-suru 93

Z

zaazaa 141
zukinzukin 46
zukizuki 46, 49
zutsuu 47